Media Representations of the Cultural Other in Turkey

"Coming at a tumultuous period in modern Turkish history, when the political space for the 'other' appears to be ever-shrinking, this book provides a timely and interesting analysis of the cultural other in Turkey. Exactly who occupies the centre and how centre–periphery relations get played out in the media of TV, film, advertising, and cartoons are fascinatingly analysed by the author. This book will be of interest to scholars from a multitude of disciplines, as well as those with a general interest in Turkey's socio-political structures."
—Edel Hughes, *Middlesex University London, UK*

Alparslan Nas

Media Representations of the Cultural Other in Turkey

palgrave
macmillan

Alparslan Nas
Marmara University
Istanbul, Turkey

ISBN 978-3-319-78345-1   ISBN 978-3-319-78346-8 (eBook)
https://doi.org/10.1007/978-3-319-78346-8

Library of Congress Control Number: 2018937510

© The Editor(s) (if applicable) and The Author(s) 2018
This work is subject to copyright. All rights are solely and exclusively licensed by the Publisher, whether the whole or part of the material is concerned, specifically the rights of translation, reprinting, reuse of illustrations, recitation, broadcasting, reproduction on microfilms or in any other physical way, and transmission or information storage and retrieval, electronic adaptation, computer software, or by similar or dissimilar methodology now known or hereafter developed.
The use of general descriptive names, registered names, trademarks, service marks, etc. in this publication does not imply, even in the absence of a specific statement, that such names are exempt from the relevant protective laws and regulations and therefore free for general use.
The publisher, the authors, and the editors are safe to assume that the advice and information in this book are believed to be true and accurate at the date of publication. Neither the publisher nor the authors or the editors give a warranty, express or implied, with respect to the material contained herein or for any errors or omissions that may have been made. The publisher remains neutral with regard to jurisdictional claims in published maps and institutional affiliations.

Cover credit: Modern building window © saulgranda/Getty

Printed on acid-free paper

This Palgrave Pivot imprint is published by the registered company Springer International Publishing AG part of Springer Nature.
The registered company address is: Gewerbestrasse 11, 6330 Cham, Switzerland

Preface

This book contributes to the scholarship on Turkey's cultural, social and political dynamics with a discussion on the depictions of the cultural other in the media particularly during the 2010s. To this purpose, I engage in a critical elaboration of the representations of the self and the other based on three films, three television series, two advertisements and various cartoons produced by different social classes between 2013 and 2018 in Turkey. The representations illustrate the diverse ways in which distinct social agents imagine their relationships with their cultural other. The notions of the center and the periphery provide crucial strategies for these social agents to realize themselves vis-à-vis the cultural other.

Turkey's modern history has been characterized by a particular tension between the social classes occupying the "center" of society—representing the bureaucratic state elite with modern, Westernized, secular and Turkish identity—and the peripheral communities representing conservative, religious and non-Turkish identities. Turkey's recent past since the turn of the century shows that the political representatives of peripheral/conservative social classes are marching to society's center. However, in this book I aim to facilitate a timely intervention to problematize this possible perception and highlight the complex dynamics of center–periphery relations through the representation of the cultural other in the media. In this respect, I argue that the notions of the center and the periphery do not signify stable positions occupied by certain social classes, rather they involve a dynamic and complex interplay of power relations exercised by different social agents who tend to identify themselves with a superior position of a centered self and define their relations to the peripheral cultural other. The field of media perfectly illustrates the complex interplay of power relations exercised by different social classes who imagine themselves at the center and discursively establish the cultural other through film, television, advertising and cartoons.

Based on a cultural studies perspective, I hope this book will provide useful insights for researchers from various disciplines including anthropology, media studies, sociology and political science, who are willing to pursue original research questions about Turkey's contemporary political, social and cultural dynamics.

I would like to thank Senior Commissioning Editor Lina Aboujieb and Editorial Assistant Ellie Freedman from Palgrave Macmillan for their invaluable guidance during the book's production process. The comments from anonymous reviewers greatly contributed to this research by helping me organize my thoughts with new perspectives and develop arguments in a more efficient way. I am thankful to Dr. Murat Akser from Ulster University, Dr. Kathleen Cavanaugh from National University of Ireland, Galway and Dr. Edel Hughes from Middlesex University London for their support and kind endorsements. Finally, I am grateful to my beloved partner, Hülya, for her endless emotional and intellectual support throughout this process.

Istanbul, Turkey   Alparslan Nas

Contents

1 Introduction: Locating the Cultural Other in Turkey
  Through a Center–Periphery Dichotomy   1

2 The Cultural Other in Film Narratives: Gendered
  Perspectives   27

3 The Making of a Militarized Self and the Other
  in Television Series: A Reformulation of the Center?   49

4 New Cultural Others? Unveiling the Limitations
  and Paradoxes   71

5 Toward a Conclusion: Imagining the Cultural Other   91

Bibliography   97

Index   105

List of Figures

Fig. 4.1 A misogynistic cartoon by *Misvak*. (Retrieved from https://www.facebook.com/misvakdergi/photos/a.1668212910067998.1073741829.1668161890073100/2006184012937551/?type=3 on February 8, 2018) 83

Fig. 4.2 "White Toros" cartoon. (Retrieved from "*Misvak* put Erdoğan on White Toros for Conquest" http://www.diken.com.tr/misvak-erdogani-beyaz-torosa-bindirip-fetihe-cikardi/ on February 7, 2018) 86

Fig. 4.3 Speciesism in a *Misvak* cartoon. (Retrieved from https://www.facebook.com/misvakdergi/photos/a.1668170840072205.1073741828.1668161890073100/2011868162369136/?type=3&theater on February 8, 2018) 87

CHAPTER 1

Introduction: Locating the Cultural Other in Turkey Through a Center–Periphery Dichotomy

Abstract This chapter introduces an historical overview of Turkey's center–periphery conflict to shed light on the ways in which the cultural other is represented in Turkey. Starting from the political and historical conditions that constitute this phenomenon, the chapter explores Turkey's last two decades, particularly focusing on the era of Justice and Development Party (JDP) governments since 2002 from a center–periphery perspective. The analysis and the discussion provided in this chapter argue that center–periphery relations are important not only in understanding Turkey's political processes, but also in problematizing the ways in which the other is depicted in a cultural sphere, particularly in media representations. Since the foundation of the Turkish nation-state in 1923, social and political processes have been characterized with the conflicting relations between the center and the periphery. The center represents the country's Republican, secular and bureaucratic elite that aims to modernize society, whereas the periphery refers to the social and cultural differences associated with religious, pro-Islamist, conservative and Kurdish communities residing at the periphery, who resist the newly founded secular nation-state's modernization efforts in varying ways. The analysis of contemporary media representations of the cultural other in Turkey points out the diverse interplay of power relations exercised by different social agents, who imagine the periphery as the cultural other from distinct perspectives.

Keywords Turkish history • Turkish politics • JDP (AKP) • Power relations • Orientalism • Media

1.1 The Origins of Center–Periphery Relations

The relations between the center and the periphery have been greatly influential in shaping past and contemporary political and social developments as well as discourses on the self and the other in Turkey. The terms were first applied to the Turkish context by sociologist Şerif Mardin in "Center–Periphery Relations: A Key to Turkish Politics?" published in 1973. In his article, Mardin engages in an historical periodization of center–periphery relations which date from the pre-modern stages of the Ottoman Empire to the modern Republic of Turkey in the mid-twentieth century. According to Mardin, the initial tensions between the society's center and its periphery were established between the Ottoman Sultan and his officials and Anatolia's segmented societies since the pre-modern and early modern periods (Mardin 1973, p. 171). Center–periphery relations during the Ottoman Empire entered a new stage in the nineteenth century, when Ottoman officials undertook reforms for modernization in the course of establishing a nation-state. During this period, modernization attempts constituted a strong bureaucratic center as the core of the nation-state that sought to achieve further social transformation: the integration of non-Muslims and peripheral populations to Ottoman nation-state identity (Mardin 1973, p. 175).

The creation of a bureaucratic elite as well as the development of a military and an intellectual generation, which maintained close ties with the French tradition of nation-state building, paved the way for the decline of absolute monarchy, which ended in 1908 with the Young Turk Revolution and the establishment of the constitution (Mardin 1971, p. 201). Between 1908 and 1918, the Young Turk movement continued its attempts at modernization and the empowerment of the nation-state based on Turkish nationalism (Zürcher 2004, p. 3). Yet this period was marked by a series of traumas experienced by the Empire, particularly with the loss of Balkan territories during the Balkan Wars (1912–1913) and Middle Eastern lands during World War I (1914–1918). During this period, the periphery was a geographical region that the Empire clung to with insistent and costly efforts, a process that ended up with the partitioning of the Empire by the Allies after World War I. This era also signified a transformation in defining the periphery. With the separation of many of its non-Muslim and non-Turkish populations of the Empire, including the Arabs, Armenians and Greeks, Anatolia remained as the central locus for a potential resistance. Eventually, with the occupation of Istanbul in 1918, the central government lost its effectiveness and an alternative national parliament was established in Ankara, which organized the National War of Independence against the occupation of Anatolia (1919–1922). Led by Mustafa Kemal Atatürk, the national struggle managed to defeat the Allies troops, which resulted in the Treaty of Lausanne in July 1923, determining modern Turkey's political territories, and paving the way for the declaration of the Republic on October 23, 1923. By this time, the 623-year-old monarchy had already been removed (in November 1922), a revolutionary step reflecting the government's goals to constitute a modern and a secular democracy.

1.2 New Dynamics of Center–Periphery Conflict in the Republican Era

With the dissolution of the Ottoman Empire, the definitions of the center and the periphery were somehow inherited by the newly founded Republic, whose political dynamics were, to a great extent, dominated by the inclinations toward the cultural other. In the early stages of the Republic, there existed two major political groups in the national assembly: the Republican People's Party (RPP) led by Mustafa Kemal Atatürk, and the "Second Group," which consisted of diverse political and regional members opposing RPP's secularist tendencies with a religious emphasis (Mardin 1973, p. 180). The Second Group was soon mobilized in the Progressive Republican Party, which was shut down for promoting religious fundamentalism and supporting the Kurdish independence movement after the Kurdish Sheikh Said Rebellion in 1925 (Jenkins 2008, p. 103). The following years solidified Kemalism as the state's official ideology, characterized by a state-imposed set of reforms to create a secular, Western-type society (Yavuz 2003, p. 31), with various reform acts including the admission of the civil code, inspired by the Swiss code, in 1926 (Arat 2010, p. 39) and the alphabet reform that switched the Arabic script to Latin in 1928 (Hurd 2009, p. 66). Attempting to establish democracy with a multi-party system, Atatürk encouraged the foundation of an opposition party in 1930, the Liberal Republican Party. After the Menemen Incident that took place in Izmir, resulting in an uprising of religious fundamentalists murdering a Turkish soldier named Kubilay, the party was considered as a potential alternative through which anti-Kemalist ideology could mobilize and was consequently shut down (Azak 2010, p. 21). The country was ruled by RPP governments until 1950 when the Democrat Party (DP) was victorious in elections, changing the government after a 27-year reign (Carkoglu and Kalaycioglu 2009, p. 18).

The political and social tensions of the early Republican era were greatly influenced by the center–periphery dichotomy. According to Mardin (1973, p. 183), during this era the Kemalists' core aim was to strengthen the center over the periphery in order to regain the state's power to actualize radical transformations on the social sphere. In this regard, the RPP elite failed to connect with the peripheral populations. Although the party acknowledged peasants as "fundamental Turks" with historical values and traditions that they continue with, the RPP focused on reproducing symbols of national identity rather than transforming the welfare conditions of the periphery (Mardin 1973, p. 183). According to the Kemalist elite, religion was a notion whose public visibility posed a threat to the country's modernization, therefore they attempted a top to bottom modernization to eliminate the potential harm of religious lifestyles (Karasipahi 2008, p. 20). Various policies were enacted, particularly after 1930, toward development and industrialization of agriculture with state-centered planning, yet these efforts remained limited and the cultural barriers between the center and the periphery persisted basically due to the religious discourse. Signified by the Sheikh Said Rebellion and the Menemen Incident, the periphery was considered as a potential threat to Kemalist modernization as it was associated with backwardness, religious fundamentalism and, in the case of Turkey's south-eastern provinces, Kurdish separatism (Yavuz 2003, p. 139).

Within this dichotomy between the "whiteness" of the center as opposed to the "blackness" of the periphery (Rosati 2015, p. 85; Yumul 2010, p. 362), the center as represented by the RPP and Kemalism attempted a top-down modernization with a series of attempts at Westernization, which included the shutdown of madrasas (religious schools) and tariqas (Dervish lodges) (Azak 2010, p. 10); changes in traditional clothing style; the alphabet reform; the translation of the Quran into Turkish; citing the call for prayer (ezan) in Turkish instead of Arabic (Azak 2010, p. 45); and changes to the civil code regarding marital relations that grant women equal rights with men. These social transformations resulted in the disillusionment of the peripheral populations in terms of their relationship with central government. The periphery was the cultural other that maintained a threatening presence, yet at the same time it was the focus of Kemalist imagination as a distant phenomenon, waiting to be transformed, enlightened and empowered. Paradoxically, Anatolia and the periphery constituted the core identity of the Turkish nation, yet needed to be modernized so that this area could be properly integrated into national identity and reach its potential.

Extending Mardin's analysis regarding center–periphery relations as key to Turkish politics, I argue that center–periphery relations and, remarkably, the periphery itself, have been widely influential in the circulation of cultural discourses that shaped the definitions of the self and the other. Since the early Republican era, the center's (namely the Kemalist ideology's) superiority has been depicted through the imagination of the periphery in various narratives, ranging from literature to social sciences and music. Various authors including Ömer Seyfettin, Halide Edip Adıvar, Refik Halit Karay and Yakup Kadri Karaosmanoğlu problematized the center's relations to the periphery in their work since the late Ottoman Empire and the early Republican period while the process of nation-building was taking place. One of the most symbolic discourses of this era was manifest in Ahmet Kutsi Tecer's poem, "Orada bir köy var uzakta / o köz bizim köyümüzdür / gezmesek de tozmasak da / o köy bizim köyümüzdür" ["There is a village distant out there / that village is our village / even if we do not go there / that village is our village"], a work that has become one of the canonical texts in Turkish national literature (Ahiska 2010, p. 63). The imagination of the cultural other through the periphery was also manifest in Atatürk's famous words, "Köylü milletin efendisidir" ["the peasants are the masters of the nation"], which attempt to narrow the distance between the center and the periphery. In addition, the early Republican industrial efforts, including the construction of railways throughout the country, were considered to be a sign of the center's endeavor to connect with the periphery. As the famous lyrics of the 10th Year March of the Republic claim, "Demir ağlarla ördük anayurdu dört baştan" ["We knitted the motherland all across with iron networks"]. This signified the center's insistence on sustaining an increased connectivity with the periphery, so that it could be included in the national whole. Radio broadcasting during the early Republican period precisely illustrates Kemalism's intentions to convey a particular image of the nation to its citizens (Ahiska 2010, p. 20). The prominent discourses of this era signified the manifestation of the cultural other through an imagination directed toward the peripheral subjectivity. Within this relation, the periphery was largely deprived of the means to express itself. It was rather discursively established by the privileged agents of the center and was instrumental in the constitution of a coherent, consistent and powerful national identity located at the center.

1.3 The Growing Visibility of the Periphery in Multi-Party Era

The relations between the center and the periphery began to transform with the foundation of the DP in 1946. Consisting of former members of the RPP, including Celal Bayar and Adnan Menderes, the DP emerged victorious in the 1950 elections, winning 83% of the seats in parliament. The comprehensive victory of the DP was considered to be the periphery's reaction against the RPP's 27-year reign, as the new era signaled promises to bring services to peasants, de-bureaucratize the state and liberalize religious practices (Azak 2010, p. 74; Mardin 1973, p. 184). According to Mardin (1973, p. 186), this new era in politics unfolded a new dichotomy reflected in parliament, where the RPP represented the bureaucratic center as opposed to the DP, which represented the democratic periphery.

The DP era was largely characterized by populist cultural policies based on religion, distancing from the RPP's statist policies by the privatization of industries and a national security concern, which found its best expression through an anti-communist propaganda. This period involved the undoing of the RPP's policies toward the periphery, notably with the termination of "Köy Enstitüleri" ["Village Institutes"] (Fortna 2010, p. 21) and "Halkevleri" ["People's Houses"] which were two prominent institutions that aimed to transform the periphery by integrating them into Kemalism's modern and secular project (Kaya 2013, p. 43). Following the DP's two consecutive election victories in 1954 and 1957, the party was removed from power in May 1960 as a result of a military coup, which culminated in capital punishment for Prime Minister Adnan Menderes (Zürcher 2004, p. 248). The military coup and the execution of the DP leader were traumatic events for the periphery, whose rise to center was forcibly prevented by the military junta, which aimed to restore the country to its original establishment.

The following periods in Turkey witnessed the resurgence of the periphery through political parties succeeding the DP tradition. Remarkably, the

Justice Party (JP) won subsequent elections in 1964 and 1969 under the leadership of Süleyman Demirel (Carkoglu and Kalaycioglu 2009, p. 3). Known as the "Çoban Sülü" [Shepherd Süleyman], Demirel's persona represented an ordinary villager's rise to power (Yavuz 2003, p. 65). The 1970s were also characterized by rapid industrialization and the development of metropolitan areas in Istanbul and Ankara due to flows of migration from Anatolia (Yavuz 2003, p. 85). By the 1980s, urban centers such as Istanbul and Ankara were heavily populated by Anatolian people, who migrated to industrial areas for work, leading to increased conflict between the center and the periphery based on social inequalities and economic disparities (White 2010, p. 435). Interrupted by another military coup in September 1980, the periphery's march to political power continued throughout the 1980s when Turgut Özal's Motherland Party (MP) succeeded the JP's hegemony in center-right politics, addressed the peripheral bourgeoisie and attempted privatization of the economy, which led to the consolidation of the free market with the intrusion of multi-national companies (Navaro-Yashin 2002, p. 223). The Özal era marked Turkey's integration into the global economy as well as the media world with the establishment of private radio and television channels (Öncü 2010, p. 390). In this period, Özal created a television persona based on expressing his piety in public, which was a clear attempt to connect with the religious masses in the periphery (Jenkins 2008, p. 149).

In the meantime, political Islam, which was forwarded by Necmettin Erbakan with his National Order Party during the 1970s, increased its power as an alternative peripheral force in politics in the post-1980 era (Çınar and Duran 2008, p. 149; White 2002, p. 192). Erbakan won the election and became prime minister in 1996 with his "Welfare Party" (WP). This was a political development that met with harsh reaction from the military, once again ending up with February 28 military memorandum—a decision taken by the National Security Council on February 28, 1997 accusing Erbakan's party of anti-secular activities (Jenkins 2008, p. 162). The process once again introduced a military intervention in politics, signifying the Republican center's attempt to restore the official ideology against the rise of Islamism (Cizre-Sakallioglu and Cinar 2003, p. 316; Kaya 2013, p. 164; Kuzmanovic 2012, p. 10). Erbakan was forced to resign in June 1997 and was replaced by the leader of the MP, Mesut Yılmaz. In June 1998, the WP was banned from politics by Turkey's Constitutional Court for being involved in anti-secular activities (Yavuz 2003, p. 247). In the meantime, the WP had been successful in the 1994 local elections, which resulted in its victory in metropolitan areas such as Istanbul and Ankara. The WP's success was significant for political Islam's rise to the center in the sense that it was the first time in Turkey's political history that the country's largest urban areas were governed by Islamist mayors, including Recep Tayyip Erdoğan in Istanbul. In 1999, Erdoğan was sentenced to ten months' imprisonment and banned from politics for promoting religious hatred due to a poem that he cited at one of his rallies (Jenkins 2008, p. 166). As influential political figures of the Islamist movement, Erbakan and Erdoğan's sentences signified the center's oppressive tendency to reassert the Republican ideology against the periphery, which was considered a threat to the central establishment.

1.4 Center–Periphery Relations in the 2000s: A Turning Point?

In the late 1990s and the early 2000s, Erdoğan emerged as a popular political figure with increasing public support, as he also represented an opposition to the traditionalist establishment within Islamist politics symbolized by Erbakan's persona (Aydın and Dalmıs 2008, p. 202; Yıldız 2008, p. 43). Different from Erbakan's anti-Western and anti-capitalist political impulses, Erdoğan came up with an alternative political movement that aimed to reconcile Islam with Western notions of democracy and liberal economy by claiming that they "took off the national outlook shirt," signifying their departure from traditional Islamist politics by means of the moderation of Islamism (Cevik 2015, p. 19; Mardin 2005, p. 160). Declaring his political position as a "conservative democrat," Erdoğan has been the founder and the first leader of the JDP in 2001 (Axiarlis 2014, p. 80; Çayır 2008, p. 74; Cevik 2015, p. 54; Duran 2008, p. 82). Winning its first election soon after it was founded in November 2002 with 34% of the vote, the JDP managed to win the majority of seats in parliament that would enable it to form a single-party government. The party's main policies had an increasing emphasis on privatization of the economy, resulting in Turkey's annual growth rate of 5–10% between the years 2002 and 2008, which was complemented by the government's attempts toward European Union membership and achieved the launch of accession negotiations on October 3, 2005 (Bardakci et al. 2017, p. 4).[1] The JDP's integration into the global

---

[1] "GDP growth (annual %)" World Bank. Available: https://data.worldbank.org/indicator/NY.GDP.MKTP.KD.ZG?locations=TR, accessed December 17, 2017.

economy as well as the steps it took toward modernization of the country, particularly with reference to liberties in the EU accession period, were remarkable achievements that led to the appreciation of the JDP as the country's democratizing power by reconciling Islamism with modern democracy (Cevik 2015, p. 71).

Since the party's election victory in 2002, Erdoğan systematically positioned himself as the representative of the peripheral populations who had been left out of Turkey's modern and elite center since the foundation of the Republic. During this period, the JDP maintained a "discursive coalition" with secular, liberal and leftist groups that were critical against the militarist tendencies of the Republic's official ideology (Erol et al. 2016, p. 5). In one of his speeches in 2005, for the first time Erdoğan declared that the party should be seeking a peaceful solution to Turkey's Kurdish issue (Kaya 2013, p. 110), which had been going on since 1984, with armed conflicts between the Turkish Army and the Kurdistan Worker's Party (PKK) (Kaya 2013, p. 103). Aiming to solve Turkey's ongoing Kurdish issue, present since the foundation of the nation-state, JDP officials announced the beginning of the "Democratic Initiative Process" or the "Kurdish Opening" in 2009, which included a series of peace negotiations with the Kurdish community (Axiarlis 2014; Bardakci et al. 2017, p. 6; Kaya 2013, p. 111). The process signified a potential turning point in modern Turkey's history, with the possibility of establishing a democratic reformulation based on the notions of equal citizenship, identities, pluralism and multi-culturalism. Moreover, it was a definite signal regarding the transformation of boundaries between the center and the periphery; as the rights of the Kurdish community (identified as the peripheral other by the Republican ideology) had been in the process of being recognized by the country's other peripheral representative in politics.

Besides the steps taken toward the solution of the Kurdish issue, the JDP era also marked the increasing visibility of Turkey's religious populations in society and politics. During its reign, the party aimed to democratize law and civil society by attempting to lift the bans on and stereotypes of the Muslim way of life in civil society and state institutions. The replacement of the bureaucratic center with government-affiliated social classes and the lifting of the "headscarf ban" which, after the February 27, 1997 coup, prohibited veiled women from entering universities and being employed in state institutions, have been the party's primary goals (Cevik 2015, p. 59; Çınar 2008, p. 117). The ban pointed out the gendered dynamics of center–periphery conflict, a discrimination against women, as the headscarf was considered by the Republican elite as a symbol of backwardness and a threat to modernization (Göle 1996, 1997). The growing visibility of the headscarf highlighted the threat associated with the periphery, indicating its march to the center (Sayan-Cengiz 2016, p. 37).

During this period, the JDP was frequently accused of religious fundamentalism by the proponents of official Republican ideology. Secularist rallies in 2007 protested Abdullah Gül's presidential candidacy based on his Islamist identity and his wife Hayrünnisa Gül's veiling. The JDP also met an "e-intervention" in 2007 in an online declaration of the army warning that the party was becoming the center of religious fundamentalism (Kaya 2013, p. 64). Furthermore, an attempt by the Constitutional Court to shut down the party took place in 2008, which was dramatically declined with high court judges voting six against and five for (Axiarlis 2014, p. 72). The headscarf ban in universities was de facto cancelled in 2010 (Kaya 2013, p. 159), yet it remained at state institutions and could not be lifted until October 2013, and in February 2017, the ban was finally lifted for army officers (Köylü 2017).[2] The first veiled female members of parliament could only be elected in the June 2015 general elections (Hurtas 2015), which was a political breakthrough in Turkey. Despite the fact that the headscarf controversy has essentially been the symbol of Islamist politics (Islam 2010, p. 64), the reason why it took so long to be solved was due to the JDP's struggle to finally maintain full hegemony over state institutions after 13 years of its reign. Although the JDP has formed single-party governments since 2002 and it seemed that it was in charge of state affairs, it was not until the mid-2010s when the party's progress eventually marked the consolidation of the peripheral political agent within the state institution.

As the peripheral social class represented by the JDP consolidated its dominance politically by the 2010s, the government met with increasing criticism of the party's switch from democratization toward authoritarianism (Öniş 2015; Somer 2016). In this regard, the Gezi Park protests in June 2013 and the way that they were suppressed by the government has been considered as a crucial indicator of the JDP's authoritarian tendencies (Gürcan and Peker 2015, p. 7; Ünan 2015, p. 85; Yalcintas 2015, p. 3).

[2] "Türkiye'de başörtüsü yasağı: Nasıl başladı, nasıl çözüldü?" [The veiling ban in Turkey: How did it start, how was it solved?] Al Jazeera Turk. Available: http://www.aljazeera.com.tr/dosya/turkiyede-basortusu-yasagi-nasil-basladi-nasil-cozuldu, accessed December 17, 2017.

This era also marked the party's distancing from Western ideals as JDP officers frequently accused "the West" of attempting to hinder Turkey's economic development by provoking social movements (Mercan and Özşeker 2015, p. 108). As anti-Western sentiment grew and became integrated into the JDP's mainstream political discourse, parallel developments took place, including the assertion of discourses and policies promoting Islamic lifestyles in civil society and education, through which the government projected its own cultural agenda onto society (Axiarlis 2014, p. 196). In one of his public speeches, Erdoğan declared that "they want to raise pious generations," a discourse that he has repeated since then, meeting with the criticisms of the country's secular Republican social classes (Lüküslü 2016, p. 637; Özbudun 2014, p. 157). This period also marked the discussions on the country's increased polarization, between Erdoğan's followers consisting of conservative social classes and the oppositional secular segments of society (Atay 2013). On the other hand, the fall of the Kurdish opening in July 2015 and the beginning of armed struggles greatly traumatized the country's democratic achievement and once again put the periphery on the agenda as a threatening space that needed to be overcome.

1.5 Media Representations of the Peripheral Other: An Historical Overview

Radio

Media representations in Turkey have been greatly influenced by center–periphery relations since the foundation of the nation-state. Since the early Republican period, radio has been an influential tool for the newly founded state to reach out to citizens, particularly to the peripheral other, in order to construct a national identity (Ahiska 2010, p. 65; Öncü 1995, p. 55). During this period, radio broadcasting projected a certain image of the nation, communicating from the center to the periphery and functioning as an ideological state apparatus that helped constitute the discourse on national self and identity.

Film

The post-World War II period witnessed the growth of the film industry, during which traditional Turkish cinema industry and language (coined as the "Yeşilçam" [Green Pine]) was established, particularly from the 1960s onwards. Between the 1960s and 1990s, Yeşilçam generated various actresses, actors, directors and films seen by millions of citizens around the country, until television finally challenged film's dominance as a popular medium of story-telling in the 1990s. This golden age of Turkish cinema involved various directors, such as Ömer Lütfi Akad, Ertem Eğilmez, Atıf Yılmaz and Yılmaz Güney, who frequently dealt with the conflicts between the center and the periphery in their films. Based on religious, cultural, classed or gendered dynamics, many films problematized the center's relation to periphery as well as the periphery itself.

Since the 1960s, the frequently depicted themes included suburban poverty as well as the oppressive feudal dynamics in the periphery in the forms of drama and comedy. During this period, various films depicted the alienation and the frustration of the peripheral individual in the urban center due to economic and social problems of adjustment (Öncü 2000, p. 305). The representations of the cultural other continued with "New Turkish Cinema" after the 1980s (Akser and Bayrakdar 2014; Atam 2009, p. 202; Suner 2010), shaped by a distinctive cinematic language that engages in symbolic expressions of identity, social trauma, remembrance of the past as well as the imaginations of the peripheral men and women in the films of several filmmakers including Nuri Bilge Ceylan, Zeki Demirkubuz and Yeşim Ustaoğlu (Suner 2010). New Turkish Cinema also included various efforts by filmmakers to undertake a rereading of Turkey's political history based on multi-culturalism, extending the peripheral inquiry to Turkey's non-Muslim populations who were forced to migrate between the 1920s and 1960s as a result of the nationalist project (Karanfil 2006; Koksal 2016; Suner 2009, p. 72).

Cartoons

Cartoon magazines also included various depictions of the peripheral other from the 1940s onwards in the figure of *Hacıağa*, connoting a male, rich landowner in the periphery invading Istanbul with his fake piousness and uncultivated manners (Öncü 1999, p. 100). In the 1960s and 1970s, the *Arabesk* culture was a prominent theme of cartoon magazines (Öncü 1999, p. 104), pointing out the inappropriateness posed by the hybrid identity of the peripheral subject migrated to Istanbul. Originating from the music of singers such as Ibrahim Tatlıses and Orhan Gencebay, who came to Istanbul from peripheral towns and achieved huge success, the *Arabesk* implies a synthesis between Western and Eastern tones of musical performance. It was the music of the suburban other who migrated to the metropolitan area and was struggling to adjust to modern urban life (Özbek 1991; Stokes 1992). By the 1990s, the suburban other had been depicted in cartoons ever more boldly with the term *Maganda*, another invader figure who "pollutes and infects" the urban self with his inappropriateness and uncultivated behavior (Öncü 1999, p. 111). It should also be noted that weekly satirical cartoon magazines such as *Gırgır, Limon, Hıbır* and *Leman* were reaching 1.5 million young readers every month (Öncü 1999, p. 111), hence dominating the discourses of the other as media representations.

Television

As another popular and influential medium, television in Turkey was introduced in 1964 with the foundation of the government channel Turkish Radio and Television (TRT). Yet television only became the mainstream news and entertainment medium in the 1990s with the liberalization of the Turkish economy during the 1980s and the initiation of private television channels in 1989. Until this period, film, newspapers and radio were the primary media that shaped public opinion, as well as the perceptions of the self and other. During the 1970s, television particularly functioned as the official voice of the state, where Islam or any other peripheral agent was absent from televisual discourse (Öncü 1995, p. 56). The era of television after the 1990s paved the way for different social classes to manifest themselves and their causes in this medium, including Islamist and Kurdish broadcasting (Öncü 2000, p. 307; Sinclair and Smets 2014, p. 324; Smets 2016, p. 3; Yavuz 2003, p. 10). However, the powerful media corporations in the 1990s were dominated by secular business owners, who maintained close ties with Republican ideology and the military class. Therefore, television had a profound impact on the construction of social realities by these business owners, significantly in relation to two main peripheral subjects, the Kurds and the Islamists (Yesil 2016, p. 51). During this period, television was influential in disseminating the official discourses of the Republic. Nonetheless, various personalities belonging to Islamist or Kurdish peripheral social classes occasionally appeared on television channels, reaching out to audiences. Despite the possibilities provided by this medium, television predominantly remained the primary tool for Republican secularist ideology, such that the February 28, 1997, coup has been renamed "the post-modern coup," highlighting the role television plays in shaping social reality by its systematic broadcasts warning viewers about the rise of Islamic fundamentalism (Toprak 2005, p. 175). In addition to the news discourse on television, soap operas and advertisements from this era were also dominated by a certain imagery conveying mainstream signifiers related to the country's secular Turks; excluding any associations that would represent the lives and images of different religious or cultural identities.

Advertising

Advertising in Turkey constitutes a crucial field dominated by totalizing discourses on the self and the other. Developed throughout the 1960s and 1970s, the growth of the advertising industry reflected the country's transformation into a consumer society. Advertisements gained a prominent role in the visualization of cultural experience in the 1980s, using culture as a reservoir of meanings to convey the brands' promises through representations of certain lifestyles (Gürbilek 2011, p. 21). During this era, the industry was largely formed by advertisers who were part of leftist and secular social classes, whose worldviews were reflected on advertising images. Eventually, advertisements turned television into a mirror that reflected normative comprehensions of culture where a secular lifestyle constituted the normative domain representation. As ideological narratives reproducing hegemonic cultural meanings (Williamson 1985), advertisements depict dominant representations of gender, race and class; as in the case of Turkey, they are discourses that systematically exclude any images that would signify various religious, cultural or classed identities. Such discursive dynamics persisted in the JDP era and, despite transformations in the political sphere, the peripheral subjectivities were not represented in advertising as its imagery was still being dominated by secular signifiers that constituted the normative basis of Turkish culture (Yel and Nas 2014). Hence advertisements constitute an authoritative realm of discourses that exclude any semantic elements that would signify the other, including various religious and cultural identities as well as those of the lower classes.

Journalism

As the JDP was successful in subsequent elections and consolidated its power throughout the 2000s, the party's dominant political discourse asserted its presence particularly in the discourses of news broadcasting.

The 2000s witnessed the JDP's attempts to cultivate a loyal media for its political ambitions (Yesil 2016, p. 91). After 2002, several important television channels and newspapers including *Akşam*, Show TV, *Star*, Star TV, *Vatan*, Kanaltürk, *Sabah*, ATV, Bugün TV, which were previously owned by secularist/Republican media owners, were interfered with by the government, and ownership was given to JDP-affiliated business owners (Yesil 2016, pp. 89–90). Apart from these media outlets and the ones with organic ties to the JDP, such as *Yeni Şafak* and *Yeni Akit*; NTV, Kanal D, CNN Türk, *Milliyet* and *Vatan* owned by Doğan, Demirören and Doğuş Holdings were not organically tied to the JDP but were considered as paying homage to the JDP's principles. In March 2018, Doğan Media Company was sold to Demirören Group, which was considered as an outcome of government's pressure against Doğan, who was in control of the highest circulating dailies *Posta* and *Hürriyet*, as well as TV channels Kanal D and CNN Türk (Coskun 2018). *Sözcü*, *Cumhuriyet*, *Birgün* and *Evrensel* newspapers constitute the media outlets that are openly anti-government, in addition to television channels such as Halk TV and Tele 1, which are small enterprises compared to the size of JDP-dominated media outlets (Akgül 2015). Other than these corporations, FOX TV is owned by US media company News Corporation, which began its operation in Turkey in 2007 and is regarded as positioning itself as a secularist media portal occasionally criticizing government policies.

There is no doubt that the transformation in media ownership in the last decade highlights the periphery's march to the center and its consolidation of power. The current situation in Turkey embodies a peculiar experience of the media where it is uncommon for one to encounter a news item that is anti-government in television channels and newspapers. However, one needs to distinguish between the journalistic field and the cultural field to be able to uncover the complex dynamics of the representation of the self and the other in the media. In this regard, I observe that while the government's ideology dominates the news discourse, the peripheral, conservative, religious lifestyles are underrepresented in various media such as film, television, advertising and cartoons, which are to a large extent dominated by the signifiers of a secularist, modernist, Turkish and centrist imagination toward the peripheral other. Although this may be related to the Republican cultural capital dominating the peripheral agent, which lacks the necessary cultural capital in the sphere of cultural representations and production (Sanli 2015, p. 15), the situation also highlights that the media constitute a diversity of discourses to which different social agents participate to define, set up or negotiate the boundaries between the self and the other in varying degrees.

1.6 Research Methodology and Theoretical Framework

The conflict between the center and the periphery has been a crucial element in the shaping of Turkey's political and social processes. Over the past 15 years, the JDP, as the representative of the periphery, established its political hegemony by winning five general elections in 2002, 2007, 2011 and 2015, three local elections in 2004, 2009 and 2014, and three referendums in 2007, 2010 and 2017. The party's political achievements may lead to a certain presumption that center–periphery relations are transforming in Turkey and that the periphery has moved to the center. While I acknowledge that undoubtedly the periphery managed to establish a substantial amount of political power, I argue that that this era also signifies a crisis of cultural hegemony, which is reflected in the sphere of popular culture, particularly with media representations. Despite the significant transformations in center–periphery relations in the JDP era, I observe that the periphery's rise to the center has largely remained as a political project imposed from above by its political power, lacking sufficient cultural basis.

Contemporary media representations show that while there is a strong assertion of political influence on journalism and news, film, television series, cartoons and advertising constitute a conflicting sphere of power relations where one cannot locate clear-cut boundaries of dominance. In fact, strikingly, it can be argued that pro-Islamist or conservative social segments are underrepresented in these media narratives. It is no surprise to observe that there is a crisis of representation in the cultural sphere faced by the JDP elite, acknowledged by Erdoğan who stated that "we managed to gain political power but failed to establish cultural power" at one of his public speeches delivered in May 2017.[3] His analysis clearly illustrates that we need to problematize the sphere of culture to be able to comprehend the center–periphery relations in light of Turkey's contemporary social and political developments.

In this regard, despite the reconfigurations of the political sphere, I suggest that the notions of the center and the periphery are still useful in

---

[3] "We still have problems in social and cultural rule: President Erdoğan" May 28, 2017, Hurriyet Daily News. Available: http://www.hurriyetdailynews.com/we-still-have-problems-in-social-and-cultural-rule-president-Erdoğan-113644, accessed December 17, 2017.

analyzing the contemporary manifestations of the cultural other in Turkey throughout the 2010s. Rather than considering the center and the periphery as stable, consistent and coherent categories referring to certain identities and social classes, I prefer to treat these notions as "technologies of power" or "technologies of the self" in Michel Foucault's terms (1990, 1991, 1995) to point out the dynamic interactions and power relations between different social classes. Foucault's notion of power claims the "productive" aspect of power relations that shape and reproduce selves through the use of certain technologies, refer to the specific mechanisms of power established by discourses on the self and the other (Behrent 2013, p. 80). Center and periphery constitute certain positions, particularly in the sphere of media representations, by which one can situate oneself to exercise the technologies of the self through the initiation of a certain image on the cultural other. Similar to what Edward Said (1979) argues in *Orientalism*, the act of imagining functions as the reproduction of certain power–knowledge dynamics on the cultural other through the establishment of "imaginative geographies." Contemporary media narratives in Turkey illustrate that the representations of the periphery initiate a certain "imagination" of the cultural other exercised by diverse agents that tend to identify themselves with the privileged gaze of the center.

Based on this perspective, my purpose is to explore the possible connections between two seemingly different concepts: "imagined," which is borrowed from a social constructionist approach with specific reference to Said's work on *Orientalism*, and the "periphery," which is a sociological concept referred to by Turkish sociologist Şerif Mardin in his analysis of Turkish politics and society. Based on a cultural studies approach with a focus on media representations, I argue that these two concepts can be integrated by means of a media analysis, which will uncover the interconnections between the discourses of imagination and the periphery established and reproduced in different media such as film, cartoons, advertising and television. In this regard, the term "imagination" refers to a process that is more complex than a mere media representation; it is a way in which different social agents tend to construct a certain version of social reality and articulate their identities and privileges based on their distinction from various cultural others. As a result, the aim of this research is to show that "imagining the periphery" is not a stable act of communication or media representation that takes place between the dominant and dominated social groups in society; rather it facilitates a realm of discourse by which different social agents participate to exercise power for imagining and discursively establishing the cultural other. Eventually, the discussion provided in this book aims to contribute to our understanding of the notions of center and periphery by pointing out the dynamic boundaries between them. Furthermore, it will shed light on the contemporary ways in which different cultural others are constituted through media discourses in Turkey's political and social landscape throughout the 2010s.

1.7 Organization of Chapters

The chapters of this book are organized in order to shed light on contemporary representations of the cultural other in Turkey based on a wide array of media representations engaged by different social classes in film, television, advertising and cartoons between 2013 and 2018. With this aim, the first chapter is reserved for a discussion of contemporary film narratives, with a discussion on Deniz Gamze Ergüven's *Mustang* (2015), Yeşim Ustaoğlu's *Tereddüt* (2016) and Mustafa Fazıl Coşkun's *Yozgat Blues* (2013). These films provide crucial narratives in terms of the ways in which periphery is imagined by the directors through a gendered lens. The analysis in this chapter points out the distinct narrative strategies that the periphery, particularly its gender relations through femininities and masculinities, are represented in relation to the center. In particular, *Mustang* and *Tereddüt*, as films directed by female filmmakers, highlight the growing influence of feminist narratives in Turkish cinema after the 2000s. As traditional Turkish cinema was characterized by the silencing of women or its appropriation as an object for the male gaze, the post-1980s period witnessed the thematic transformation in the works of male and female filmmakers who frequently engaged in gender-related issues (Atakav 2012). While the total number of films directed by female filmmakers corresponds to 1.6% of all films produced by the Turkish film industry until 2002, it increased to 8.2% between 2004 and 2013 (Tanrıöver 2017, p. 5). This indicates the growing visibility of women's issues achieved by Turkey's feminist currents, which considered film as a useful medium to problematize gender relations. Since the turn of the century, gender inequality has been a prominent discussion, which also attracted the attention of mainstream media, particularly with the increasing rates of femicide, rape and violence against women across the country. In this regard, Ergüven's and Ustaoğlu's films reflect on this period's concerns of feminist filmmakers on women's subordination in Turkey's peripheral regions. On the other hand, *Yozgat Blues* is a film written and directed by a male filmmaker, Mustafa Fazıl

Coşkun, who prefers to demystify the kinds of superior meanings associated with the center with regard to the changing boundaries of masculinities and femininities, and thus tends to position the periphery as a potential venue of empowerment rather than oppression. Eventually, the analysis in this chapter will point out the diversity of narrative strategies that tend to imagine the cultural other through the depictions and the problematizations of the center–periphery dichotomy.

The third chapter focuses on three "military" television series; *Söz* [*The Promise*], *İsimsizler* [*The Nameless*] and *Savaşçı* [*The Warrior*], which began being broadcast in 2017 on Turkey's most-watched television channels, Star TV, Kanal D and FOX TV, respectively. The series share a common motive in representing the periphery as a militarized space by telling the stories of Turkish soldiers who are fighting against terrorist figures. These series can be considered as reflections of the recent political and social tendencies toward the ongoing armed struggle in the region after the breakdown of peace negotiations in 2015. Historically, Turkey's Kurdish problem has existed since the foundation of the Turkish nation-state, which excluded Kurds from the formation of a Turkish national identity (Van Bruinessen 1992). While Turkey's Kurdish issue has been critically tackled by various Kurdish filmmakers (Koçer 2013, 2014), and by television channels founded outside of Turkey such as ROJ TV (Coban 2013), the discourses in Turkish television were predominantly controlled by hegemonic meaning structures tending to reproduce the main inclinations of Turkish national identity (Toros 2012). Other than the coverage of "terror" as part of a Kurdish issue, the representation of the Kurdish community's worldviews and lifestyles are largely absent in televisual discourse, either in advertising or in television series. The only kind of representation associated with Kurds is implicitly provided as people living in the country's eastern regions, maintaining feudal and patriarchal relations and speaking in a distorted Turkish dialect. The military television series portray the Kurdish community in a similar manner; as peripheral individuals who represent the non-modern and underdeveloped cultural other as opposed to the superior self at the center, who attempts to seize hold of peripheral regions to "save" the nation and the peripheral agent from enemy figures. Finally, this chapter sheds light on the racialized imagination of the Kurdish geographies by the Turkish center by problematizing the ways in which series serve as technologies of the self that help to situate the national, militarized, Turkish self at the center.

The final chapter is reserved for a critical inquiry regarding the ways in which the government-affiliated social classes tend to imagine the other through depictions in advertising and cartoons. In this regard, it is possible to observe the limitations and the possibilities of representation conducted by the social class that was once positioned at the periphery and is now tending to secure itself a place at the center. Accordingly, this chapter points out the paradoxes of representations initiated by government-related social classes, through the analysis of two Turkish Airlines (THY) advertisements broadcast in 2014 and 2015, and *Misvak* humor magazine cartoons published in 2017. The aim of this chapter is first to problematize the ways in which THY advertisements promoting the opening of Ordu-Giresun and Iğdır airports, tend to imagine the periphery in a self-Orientalizing manner, by internalizing the already established center–periphery hierarchies. Secondly, this chapter engages in a critical analysis of cartoons published by *Misvak*, a popular humor magazine that was established in 2015 by pro-government cartoonists, to highlight the ways in which cartoons employ various discursive strategies to imagine and establish new cultural others.

Bibliography

Ahiska, M. (2010). *Occidentalism in Turkey: Questions of Modernity and National Identity in Turkish Radio Broadcasting*. London/New York: I.B. Tauris.

Akgül, E. (2015, October 29). Map of Media Ownership in Turkey. Retrieved from http://m.bianet.org/english/media/168745-map-of-media-ownership-in-turkey

Akser, M., & Bayrakdar, D. (2014). *New Cinema, New Media: Reinventing Turkish Cinema*. Newcastle upon Tyne: Cambridge Scholars Publishing.

Arat, Y. (2010). Nation Building and Feminism in Early Republican Turkey. In C. Kerslake, K. Öktem, & P. Robins (Eds.), *Turkey's Engagement with Modernity: Conflict and Change in the Twentieth Century* (pp. 38–51). London: Palgrave Macmillan.

Atakav, E. (2012). *Women and Turkish Cinema: Gender Politics, Cultural Identity and Representation*. London: Routledge.

Atam, Z. (2009). Critical Thoughts on the New Turkish Cinema. In D. Bayrakdar (Ed.), *Cinema and Politics: Turkish Cinema and the New Europe* (pp. 202–220). Cambridge: Cambridge Scholars Publishing.

Atay, T. (2013). The Clash of 'Nations' in Turkey: Reflections on the Gezi Park Incident. *Insight Turkey, 15*(3), 39–44.

Axiarlis, E. (2014). *Political Islam and the Secular State in Turkey: Democracy, Reform and the Justice and Development Party*. London/New York: I.B. Tauris.

Aydın, E., & Dalmış, I. (2008). The Social Bases of the Justice and Development Party. In Ü. Cizre (Ed.), *Secular and Islamic Politics in Turkey: The Making of the Justice and Development Party* (pp. 201–222). New York: Routledge.

Azak, U. (2010). *Islam and Secularism in Turkey: Kemalism, Religion and the Nation State.* London/New York: I.B. Tauris.

Bardakci, M., Freyberg-Inan, A., Giesel, C., & Leisse, O. (2017). *Religious Minorities in Turkey: Alevi, Armenians, and Syriacs and the Struggle to Desecuritize Religious Freedom.* London: Palgrave Macmillan.

Behrent, M. C. (2013). Foucault and Technology. *History and Technology, 29*(1), 54–104.

Carkoglu, A., & Kalaycioglu, E. (2009). *The Rising Tide of Conservatism in Turkey.* New York: Palgrave Macmillan.

Çayır, K. (2008). The Emergence of Turkey's Contemporary 'Muslim Democrats'. In Ü. Cizre (Ed.), *Secular and Islamic Politics in Turkey: The Making of the Justice and Development Party* (pp. 62–79). New York: Routledge.

Cevik, N. (2015). *Muslimism in Turkey and Beyond: Religion in the Modern World.* New York: Palgrave Macmillan.

Çınar, M. (2008). The Justice and Development Party and the Kemalist Establishment. In Ü. Cizre (Ed.), *Secular and Islamic Politics in Turkey: The Making of the Justice and Development Party* (pp. 109–131). New York: Routledge.

Çınar, M., & Duran, B. (2008). The Specific Evolution of Contemporary Political Islam in Turkey and Its 'Difference'. In Ü. Cizre (Ed.), Secular and Islamic Politics in Turkey: The Making of the Justice and Development Party (pp. 17–40). New York: Routledge.

Cizre-Sakallioglu, U., & Cinar, M. (2003). Turkey 2002: Kemalism, Islamism, and Politics in the Light of the February 28 Process. *The South Atlantic Quarterly, 102*(2), 309–332.

Coban, S. (2013). Turkey's 'War and Peace': The Kurdish Question and the Media. *Critique, 41*(3), 445–457.

Coskun, O. (2018, March 21). Pro-Erdogan Group Agrees to Buy Owner of Hurriyet Newspaper, *CNN Turk*. Retrieved from https://www.reuters.com/article/us-dogan-holding-m-a-demiroren/pro-erdogan-group-agrees-to-buy-owner-of-hurriyet-newspaper-cnn-turk-idUSKBN1GX23R

Duran, B. (2008). The Justice and Development Party's 'New Politics': Steering Toward Conservative Democracy, a Revised Islamic Agenda or Management of New Crises? In Ü. Cizre (Ed.), *Secular and Islamic Politics in Turkey: The Making of the Justice and Development Party* (pp. 80–106). New York: Routledge.

Erol, M., Ozbay, C., Turem, Z. U., & Terzioglu, A. (2016). The Making of Neoliberal Turkey: An Introduction. In M. Erol, C. Ozbay, Z. U. Turem, & A. Terzioglu (Eds.), *The Making of Neoliberal Turkey* (pp. 1–14). New York: Routledge.

Fortna, B. C. (2010). The Ottoman Educational Legacy. In C. Kerslake, K. Öktem, & P. Robins (Eds.), *Turkey's Engagement with Modernity: Conflict and Change in the Twentieth Century* (pp. 15–26). London: Palgrave Macmillan.

Foucault, M. (1990). *The History of Sexuality Volume 1: An Introduction* (trans: Hurley, R.). New York: Vintage Books.

Foucault, M. (1991). On the Genealogy of Ethics: An Overview of Work in Progress. In M. Foucault & P. Rabinow (Eds.), *The Foucault Reader* (pp. 372–340). Harmondsworth: Penguin.

Foucault, M. (1995). *Discipline and Punish: The Birth of the Prison* (trans: Sheridan, A.). New York: Vintage Books.

Göle, N. (1996). *The Forbidden Modern: Civilization and Veiling*. Ann Arbor: University of Michigan Press.

Göle, N. (1997). The Gendered Nature of the Public Sphere. *Public Culture*, 10(1), 61–81.

Gürbilek, N. (2011). Vitrinde Yaşamak: 1980'lerin Kültürel İklimi [The New Cultural Climate in Turkey: Living in a Shop Window]. Istanbul: Metis.

Gürcan, E. C., & Peker, E. (2015). *Challenging Neoliberalism at Turkey's Gezi Park: From Private Discontent to Collective Class Action*. New York: Palgrave Macmillan.

Hurd, E. S. (2009). *The Politics of Secularism in International Relations*. Princeton: Princeton University Press.

Hurtas, S. (2015, June 10). New Turkish Parliament to Be More Inclusive. Retrieved from https://www.al-monitor.com/pulse/originals/2015/06/turkey-elections-changing--portrait-of-new-parliament.html

Islam, M. K. (2010). *Headscarf Politics in Turkey: A Postcolonial Reading*. New York: Palgrave Macmillan.

Jenkins, G. (2008). *Political Islam in Turkey: Running West, Heading East?* New York: Palgrave Macmillan.

Karanfil, G. (2006). Becoming Undone: Contesting Nationalisms in Contemporary Turkish Popular Cinema. *National Identities*, 8(1), 61–75.

Karasipahi, S. (2008). *Muslims in Modern Turkey: Kemalism, Modernism and the Revolt of the Islamic Intellectuals*. London/New York: I.B. Tauris.

Kaya, A. (2013). *Europeanization and Tolerance in Turkey: The Myth of Toleration*. London/New York: Palgrave Macmillan.

Koçer, S. (2013). Making Transnational Publics: Circuits of Censorship and Technologies of Publicity in Kurdish Media Circulation. *American Ethnologist*, 40(4), 721–733. https://doi.org/10.1111/amet.12050.

Koçer, S. (2014). Kurdish Cinema as a Transnational Discourse Genre: Cinematic Visibility, Cultural Resilience, and Political Agency. *International Journal of Middle East Studies*, 46(3), 473–488.

Koksal, O. (2016). *Aesthetics of Displacement: Turkey and Its Minorities on Screen*. London/New York: Bloomsbury Publishing.

Köylü, H. (2017, February 22). TSK'da başörtüsü yasağı kalktı [Veil Ban Lifted in the Army]. Retrieved from http://www.dw.com/tr/tskda-ba%C5%9F%C3% B6rt%C3%BCs%C3%BC-yasa%C4%9F%C4%B1-kalkt%C4%B1/a-37665858
Kuzmanovic, D. (2012). *Refractions of Civil Society in Turkey*. New York: Palgrave Macmillan.
Lüküslü, D. (2016). Creating a Pious Generation: Youth and Education Policies of the AKP in Turkey. *Southeast European and Black Sea Studies, 16*(4), 637–649.
Mardin, Ş. (1971). Ideology and Religion in the Turkish Revolution. *International Journal of Middle East Studies, 2*(3), 197–211.
Mardin, Ş. (1973). Center-Periphery Relations: A Key to Turkish Politics? *Daedalus, 102*(1), 169–190.
Mardin, Ş. (2005). Turkish Islamic Exceptionalism Yesterday and Today: Continuity, Rupture and Reconstruction in Operational Codes. *Turkish Studies, 6*(2), 145–165.
Mercan, B. A., & Özşeker, E. (2015). 'Just a Handful of Looters!': A Comparative Analysis of Government Discourses on the Summer Disorders in the United Kingdom and Turkey. In A. Yalcintas (Ed.), *Creativity and Humour in Occupy Movements: Intellectual Disobedience in Turkey and Beyond* (pp. 95–115). London: Palgrave Macmillan.
Navaro-Yashin, Y. (2002). The Market for Identities: Secularism, Islamism, Commodities. In D. Kandiyoti & A. Saktanber (Eds.), *Fragments of Culture: The Everyday of Modern Turkey* (pp. 221–253). New Jersey: Rutgers University Press.
Öncü, A. (1995). Packaging Islam: Cultural Politics on the Landscape of Turkish Commercial Television. *Public Culture, 8*(1), 51–71.
Öncü, A. (1999). Istanbulites and Others: The Cultural Cosmology of 'Middleness' in the Era of Neo-liberalism. In Ç. Keyder (Ed.), *Istanbul: Between the Global and the Local* (pp. 95–119). New York: St. Martins.
Öncü, A. (2000). The Banal and the Subversive: Politics of Language on Turkish Television. *European Journal of Cultural Studies, 3*(3), 296–318.
Öncü, A. (2010). Rapid Commercialisation and Continued Control: The Turkish Media in the 1990s. In C. Kerslake, K. Öktem, & P. Robins (Eds.), *Turkey's Engagement with Modernity: Conflict and Change in the Twentieth Century* (pp. 388–402). London: Palgrave Macmillan.
Öniş, Z. (2015). Monopolising the Centre: The AKP and the Uncertain Path of Turkish Democracy. *The International Spectator, 50*(2), 22–41.
Özbek, M. (1991). Popüler kültür ve Orhan Gencebay arabeski [Popular Culture and the Arabesk of Orhan Gencebay]. Istanbul: İletişim Yayınları.
Özbudun, E. (2014). AKP at the Crossroads: Erdoğan's Majoritarian Drift. *South European Society and Politics, 19*(2), 155–167.

Rosati, M. (2015). *The Making of a Postsecular Society: A Durkheimian Approach to Memory, Pluralism and Religion in Turkey*. London/New York: Routledge.
Said, E. W. (1979). *Orientalism*. New York: Vintage Books.
Sanli, S. (2015). *Women and Cultural Citizenship in Turkey: Mass Media and 'Woman's Voice' Television*. London/New York: I. B. Tauris.
Sayan-Cengiz, F. (2016). *Beyond Headscarf Culture in Turkey's Retail Sector*. London/New York: Palgrave Macmillan.
Sinclair, C., & Smets, K. (2014). Media Freedoms and Covert Diplomacy: Turkey Challenges Europe Over Kurdish Broadcasts. *Global Media and Communication, 10*(3), 319–331.
Smets, K. (2016). Ethnic Media, Conflict, and the Nation-State: Kurdish Broadcasting in Turkey and Europe and Mediated Nationhood. *Media, Culture & Society, 38*(5), 738–754.
Somer, M. (2016). Understanding Turkey's Democratic Breakdown: Old vs. New and Indigenous vs. Global Authoritarianism. *Southeast European and Black Sea Studies, 16*(4), 481–503.
Stokes, M. (1992). *The Arabesk Debate: Music and Musicians in Modern Turkey*. Oxford: Clarendon Press.
Suner, A. (2009). Silenced Memories: Notes on Remembering in New Turkish Cinema. *New Cinemas: Journal of Contemporary Film, 7*(1), 71–81.
Suner, A. (2010). *New Turkish Cinema: Belonging, Identity and Memory*. London/New York: I.B. Tauris.
Tanrıöver, H. U. (2017). Women as Film Directors in Turkish Cinema. *European Journal of Women's Studies, 24*(4), 321–335.
Toprak, B. (2005). Islam and Democracy in Turkey. *Turkish Studies, 6*(2), 167–186.
Toros, E. (2012). The Kurdish Problem, Print Media, and Democratic Consolidation in Turkey. *Asia Europe Journal, 10*(4), 317–333.
Ünan, A. D. (2015). Gezi Protests and the LGBT Rights Movement: A Relation in Motion. In A. Yalcintas (Ed.), *Creativity and Humour in Occupy Movements: Intellectual Disobedience in Turkey and Beyond* (pp. 75–94). London: Palgrave Macmillan.
Van Bruinessen, M. (1992). Kurdish Society, Ethnicity, Nationalism and Refugee Problems. In P. G. Kreyenbroek & S. Sperl (Eds.), *The Kurds: A Contemporary Overview* (pp. 33–67). London: Routledge.
White, J. B. (2002). The Islamist Paradox. *Fragments of Culture: The Everyday of Modern Turkey* (pp. 191–221).
White, J. B. (2010). Tin Town to Fanatics: Turkey's Rural to Urban Migration from 1923 to the Present. In C. Kerslake, K. Öktem, & P. Robins (Eds.), *Turkey's Engagement with Modernity: Conflict and Change in the Twentieth Century* (pp. 425–442). London: Palgrave Macmillan.
Williamson, J. (1985). *Decoding Advertisements: Ideology and Meaning in Advertising*. London: Marion Boyars.

Yalcintas, A. (2015). Prelude: Occupy Turkey. In A. Yalcintas (Ed.), *Creativity and Humour in Occupy Movements: Intellectual Disobedience in Turkey and Beyond* (pp. 1–5). London: Palgrave Macmillan.

Yavuz, M. H. (2003). *Islamic Political Identity in Turkey*. Cary: Oxford University Press.

Yel, A. M., & Nas, A. (2014). Insight Islamophobia: Governing the Public Visibility of Islamic Lifestyle in Turkey. *European Journal of Cultural Studies, 17*(5), 567–584.

Yesil, B. (2016). *Media in New Turkey: The Origins of an Authoritarian Neoliberal State*. Urbana/Chicago/Springfield: University of Illinois Press.

Yıldız, A. (2008). Problematizing the Intellectual and Political Vestiges. In Ü. Cizre (Ed.), *Secular and Islamic Politics in Turkey: The Making of the Justice and Development Party* (pp. 41–61). New York: Routledge.

Yumul, A. (2010). Fashioning the Turkish Body Politic. In C. Kerslake, K. Öktem, & P. Robins (Eds.), *Turkey's Engagement with Modernity: Conflict and Change in the Twentieth Century* (pp. 349–369). London: Palgrave Macmillan.

Zürcher, E. J. (2004). *Turkey: A Modern History*. London/New York: I.B. Tauris.

CHAPTER 2

The Cultural Other in Film Narratives: Gendered Perspectives

Abstract This chapter discusses the different ways in which the periphery is imagined by contemporary film narratives in Turkey based on an analysis of three films, *Mustang* (2015), *Tereddüt* (2016) and *Yozgat Blues* (2013). *Mustang* is the debut film of female filmmaker Deniz Gamze Ergüven, narrating the story of five sisters facing various kinds of oppression in a village located in Turkey's Black Sea region in a conservative cultural setting. While *Mustang* undertakes a feminist critique of male-domination that subordinates the sisters, it does this by Orientalizing the peripheral other through the presence of a superior, enlightening gaze of the center. On the other hand, directed by acclaimed Turkish female film director Yeşim Ustaoğlu, *Tereddüt* highlights the mutualities between the experiences of women from different classes and cultures. Another narrative in the Black Sea region, the film tends to demystify the empowered self at the center and establishes grey zones between the center and the periphery by focusing on different women's common struggle against male domination. Finally, this chapter discusses male film director Mahmut Fazıl Coşkun's *Yozgat Blues*, to show the deconstruction of the center's masculinist, unified, superior self, challenged by the multiplicity of identities and unexpectedness of experiences promised by the periphery.

Keywords Film • Gender • Feminism • Femininities • Masculinities
• Sexuality

© The Author(s) 2018
A. Nas, *Media Representations of the Cultural Other in Turkey*,
https://doi.org/10.1007/978-3-319-78346-8_2

2.1 The Enlightening Feminist Self and the Resisting Cultural Other in *Mustang*

Exploring Women's Subordination in the Periphery

Mustang is the debut film of Turkish director Deniz Gamze Ergüven released in 2015. Written by Ergüven and Alice Winocour, it narrates the story of five young sisters living in a conservative village setting located in Turkey's Black Sea region. The film was highly acclaimed by critics around the world for addressing patriarchal relations in Anatolia with a feminist sensibility that questions women's subordination. It received an Oscar nomination from France for Best Foreign Language Film of the Year at the 2016 Academy Awards, and for Best Motion Picture—Foreign Language at the 2016 Golden Globe Awards, as well as other nominations in competitions and festivals across the globe. *Mustang* won Best First Film, Best Original Screenplay, Best Original Music and Best Editing at the César Awards 2016. It also won European Discovery of the Year Award at the European Film Awards 2015, "Audience Choice Award" at the Chicago International Film Festival 2015 and "Freedom of Expression—Honorary Award" at the CinEuphoria Awards 2017.

In Turkey, *Mustang* was released on October 23, 2015. It screened in only 16 film theaters, but was seen by 4046 viewers in the first three days of its release and by 25,419 viewers during its 22 weeks of screening, meeting with mixed responses from different Turkish film critics.[1] While some authors celebrated the film for its feminist stance on male-dominated Anatolian culture (Açar 2015; Dorsay 2015), others critically discussed the film's narration of Anatolian conservatism and the Black Sea region, pointing out that the kinds of representation shown do not fit the reality in such regions (Kural 2015; Vardan 2015). In particular, the film's portrayal of sisters in secularized outfits and showing secular behavior did not reflect the reality of the local women, most of whom use the veil as part of their traditional clothing. A third position in film critique was formed by feminist activists who celebrated the film's feminist stance, yet pointed out the inadequacies in the representation of Turkey's conservative villages, particularly by referring to the forming of an Orientalist film language (Tuncer 2016). Within this inquiry, the question was directed toward the kind of women's emancipation offered by the film, for clearly *Mustang* is

---

[1] The data is retrieved from "Box Office Turkey" website available at: https://boxofficeturkiye.com/film/mustang-2012921, accessed December 12, 2017.

a narrative of a series of conflicts and victories in women's struggles and their resistance against gendered relations of power in Turkey's Black Sea Region. As Ergüven stated in one of her interviews, the word "Mustang" means wild horses, referring to the "spirited heroines" who struggle against oppressive structures (Jones 2016). As Ergüven points out, the film's name is the initial signifier regarding the establishment of center–periphery relations in the narrative. With *Mustang*, the periphery is attributed with a certain amount of "wilderness" with the kinds of gender relations that it inhabits. Significantly, the wilderness of the periphery is situated and becomes meaningful in so far as it is positioned in contradistinction with the "civilizing" mission of the center, which is the director's superior gaze over the periphery.

Mustang narrates the experiences of five orphaned young sisters aged between 12 and 17, living in a Black Sea village with their uncle and grandmother. The film begins by portraying the start of the sisters' summer break where students leave school and wander along the coastline for fun, which sets up the primary conflict in the narrative. Soon the sisters end up joking with some boys at the seaside, getting into the water with their clothes on and engaging in horseplay with their friends. They feel free, enjoying the liberty of having fun with the boys and among themselves, without any authoritarian gaze watching them. However, on arriving home, their neighborhood has somehow been informed of their innocent interaction with the boys, and their uncle and grandmother are angry. To these authority figures, climbing on the shoulders of boys is not acceptable behavior. In their eyes, the girls have lost their virtue and therefore should be punished accordingly to get them back on the right track. Soon after this incident, the sisters ask their uncle for permission to see a football game in the nearby city of Trabzon, but he says no. The sisters then plan their escape from the house and travel to Trabzon. However, the grandmother happens to see them on television when a camera zooms in on the girls celebrating a goal. Consequently, the sisters are disciplined, dressed in traditional outfits, deprived of phones and computers, and find themselves in the position of being prepared for their future marriages.

The sequences that signal the dramatic events to come are initially depicted in the introduction by Lale, the youngest sister narrating the story, who says, "Everything changed in the blink of an eye. At first, we were comfortable, and then everything went to shit." As time goes on, the sisters feel the increasing pressure of patriarchal subordination in terms of its discursive mechanisms and bodily inspections. As the initial scenes of the film establish the patriarchal tension that will persist throughout the narrative, they also introduce the basic connotations of a center–periphery dichotomy that exerts its presence as the film's dominant theme. After Lale tells of the sharp transformation that the girls experienced, which at the same time signals the main problematic that the film promises to portray, we see Lale hugging her female teacher, Dilek. Lale is sad because Dilek is leaving town and returning to Istanbul.[2] During her emotional breakdown, Dilek tells Lale not to be upset, promising to meet the sisters and giving Lale her address. In this respect, from Lale's perspective and her interpretation of the upcoming events, the narrative implies that the oppressive events coincide with Dilek's leaving town. This particular beginning of the narrative forms the initial dichotomization of the center and the periphery; as Lale suggests, everything was fine while the teacher remained, yet traumatically transformed once the periphery was abandoned by Dilek, who is representative of the center. However, gendered forms of oppression are not dependent on a teacher being in or leaving the town; it already exists in the cultural formation at the periphery. The initial scenes metaphorically treat the teacher figure as the carrier of women's emancipation, whose absence leads to drastic changes. Established as a powerful figure inspiring Lale and her sisters to resist male domination, the impact of Dilek as the representative of the civilized and emancipated center conveys its presence throughout the narrative by empowering the sisters after the various oppressions they experience. Though not realized until the final scene of the film, Dilek represents the omnipotent presence of the center throughout the narrative, forming the girls' basic inclinations and acting as the source of the sisters' resistance.

Sexualities: A Problematic Domain for Representation

The sisters' sexuality constitutes a major area of resistance with which they counter patriarchal acts and discourses of the periphery in varying degrees. Sexuality is represented as the major area of struggle between the oppressing structures of the periphery and the sisters' resistance against them.

---

[2] According to the education system in Turkey, the state appoints newly graduated teachers to primary, secondary and high schools in peripheral provinces for mandatory service. After spending few years there, depending on the province's needs, teachers win the right to receive a promotion to larger cities.

With the initial conflict that takes place at the beginning of the film, the uncle and the grandmother decide to prepare the girls for marriage since they consider their behavior inappropriate. If they continue to act in this way, the girls will soon be stigmatized by the villagers and nobody will want to marry them. In a patriarchal setting, marriage is considered as the institution that legitimizes heterosexual intercourse. Sex is not for women's sexual pleasure, but for the purpose of reproduction and to satisfy men's sexual desire. As authority figures aiming to reproduce peripheral women's subjectivities, the uncle and grandmother effectively convert their home into a prison, not allowing the girls to go out without supervision. As the realm where the patriarchal relations of power are concentrated, the domestic sphere is disciplined with acts and discourses that aim to generate peripheral subjectivities in the sisters. At the beginning of the new academic year, the sisters are not allowed to attend school and are confined to home, which is surrounded by barriers that would prevent their escape. The grandmother and the elderly women in the neighborhood try to teach the sisters how to do different kinds of housework, however the girls are disinterested. They look for strategies to alter the peripheral disciplinary gaze of patriarchal agents. Their sexuality becomes the crucial realm where they can challenge their oppression and foster alternative identities for themselves.

Various scenes in the film depict the sisters spending time in their rooms joking with each other, talking about their experiences, dreams and ways to evade the forced marriages they may encounter at any time. In many of these sequences, the sisters are portrayed as half-naked, lying on the ground or in their beds, while the camera lingers on their bodies. From a feminist perspective, the scenes aim to convey a feeling of sisterhood, where the girls freely show autonomy over their bodies despite the oppression they encounter. However, there are two problems with this sort of sisterhood solidarity narrative. Firstly, such scenes inhabit the potential to activate the voyeuristic male gaze toward the sisters' bodies, hence contradicting the film's feminist stance. Secondly, the sisters' realization of autonomy over their bodies in these sequences may contradict the real-life experiences of peripheral women's sexuality, thus providing the audience with a distorted picture of the experiences or the challenges that these women encounter.

The film portrays the sisters as absolutely aware and in full command of their bodies. They are equipped with the necessary discourses to talk and define their sexuality and are confident in pursuing their sexual desires. Sonay, the 17-year-old sister, is a character who manages to realize sexual satisfaction with her boyfriend whom she later marries. She frequently finds a way to escape home to meet her lover and have sex. In addition, she advises her sisters to have anal sex so that they can "protect" their virginities and future marriage prospects. Although the emphasis on virginity as a patriarchal disciplinary body mechanism is closely related to the sisters' subordination, the way Sonay copes with this conflict in a confident manner by enjoying sex with her partner may not correspond to the real-life experience of a peripheral woman. This is because sex is a taboo subject in conservative regions, it is difficult to talk about and to facilitate discourses other than the ones that are imposed on women by patriarchal forms of domination. Another scene shows Lale reading a book called *My Sexual Life*, rarely a practice in rural areas where the rates of literacy are low and sex education does not exist in the school curriculum or occur within the home. Later in the film, while traveling to the town center with their uncle, one of the sisters calls her boyfriend and then has sex with him in the car with the windows open, leaving her sisters to act as lookouts. The film portrays young women who have sexual fantasies and who are self-confident despite the patriarchal culture they are exposed to. However, these scenes potentially do not fit the reality of peripheral women, who might have fantasies but are usually deprived of the means to discover or even to talk about their sexual experiences in a strict conservative setting. Aiming to focus on the sisters' resistance, the narrative falls short of providing a realistic account of how a peripheral woman might experience the complicated area of sexuality, which becomes a handicap for feminist sensibilities to correctly situate the role and the impact of sex in peripheral women's lives.

The film makes various efforts to narrate the conservatism inherent in the periphery that drastically impacts the sisters' lives. While Sonay, the eldest sister, refuses to meet the families of prospective husbands and manages to marry to her boyfriend, the other sisters are not that lucky. Selma cannot avoid a forced marriage and two of the sisters have a joint wedding. On the night of the wedding, Selma has intercourse with her husband while the mother-in-law waits outside to receive the bloodied sheet—a sign of a woman's virginity. Frustrated by the lack of any blood, the husband cannot figure out what to do, and the whole family ends up at the hospital to have Selma medically examined to establish her virginity. When the doctor asks Selma about it, she responds in a cool manner: "I have slept with everybody on earth." After the doctor tells her that she is a virgin, she replies, "No one believes me when I say I am a virgin, leave me alone." In this scene depicting a virginity examination, the woman who is being examined and disciplined under the patriarchal/medical authority is supposed to be traumatized due to the oppressive experience that she goes through. However, the scene shows Selma being very confident and resilient, fully conscious of what she is going through and able to resist. Her confidence is reflected in the sophisticated remarks she utters in her conversation with the doctor, philosophizing her condition using metaphors. This scene adds to the narrative's overall position in handling peripheral women's trauma by representing them as active, resisting subjects, rather than as victims; a strategy that may cover up the actual experiences of what a peripheral woman might go through. A similar covering up strategy is employed when Ece, the third-eldest sister, commits suicide. The narrative does not explicitly show how Ece is led to suicide, however, we understand that it is because she was raped by her uncle many times. Touching upon the problematic of incest and rape in the periphery, the film highlights the various degrees of sexual violence, without showing the processes by which a peripheral woman is traumatized by such violence.

Resistance "Imposed" on Peripheral Women

The narrative of resistance as a response to the oppressive tendencies of the periphery reaches its peak when Nur and Lale, the youngest two sisters, plan their escape from the house on the day of Nur's wedding, which is another forced marriage. While all the preparations are being completed and as Nur is about to leave the house for the wedding ceremony, Lale actualizes her plan to escape and takes Nur with her. Lale's strong character means she learns how to drive while her sisters are going through various traumas; being the youngest she almost wins time to better prepare herself for future repression. By borrowing the van of a young local man named Yasin (who likes Lale), Lale and Nur succeed in escaping after a breathtaking sequence of struggles. The final scenes of the film take place in Istanbul where the sisters arrive at their teacher's house. Dilek is surprised to see them as Lale hugs her and the film ends.

The final scene is a perfect illustration of Slovenian philosopher Slavoj Žižek's famous question with reference to Althusserian notion of ideological interpellation and Lacanian psychoanalysis: "Why does a letter always arrive at its destination?" (Žižek 2001). The film begins with Dilek's leaving town for Istanbul, handing her address to Lale, and it ends with Lale's arrival at her final destination. As the representative of an Istanbulite center, Dilek's powerful assertion to the narrative points out the presence of an ideology that exerts itself throughout the film by defining the periphery and interpellating peripheral women's subjectivities. Dilek's address is not an ordinary address in Istanbul, which has a population of 15 million and consists of various neighborhoods; Çukurcuma street near Taksim Square and Gezi Park has significance—it was the center of resistance against the government in Gezi Park activism that took place in June 2013. As the teacher, whose leaving town initiated destruction in the periphery, the narrative implies that Dilek may be an activist figure, who carries out a feminist enlightening mission over peripheral subjectivities. Indeed, despite her leaving town, her presence is felt throughout the narrative by the resisting acts of the sisters, as well as their engagement in political discourse. In several scenes we see the sisters watching news on television, where in a public speech in July 2014 the deputy prime minister says, "Women should be virtuous, should not laugh in public." In another scene, we see "resist Gezi" t-shirts in the sisters' closets—an important detail signifying the sisters' affiliation to the values embraced by Gezi activism.[3] Eventually, the film becomes a narrative by which the discourse of Gezi activism locates itself at the center and makes attempts at consciousness raising, enlightening and saving peripheral women from the patriarchal oppression that they encounter.

Mustang's references to Gezi activism and contemporary Turkish politics reveal the film's position as critical of the government, particularly apropos its remarks on gender issues. The patriarchal oppression targeting women's bodies illustrated in the film are considered as a reflection of such remarks and policies. Although it is true that government officers frequently employ sexist language, the portrayal of the periphery as being enlightened by the center represented by Gezi activism is quite problematic and may contradict a feminist sensibility. It is important to note that Gezi activism had limited impact on peripheral towns in the Black Sea region; Recep Tayyip Erdoğan won most of his votes (65%) from this region in the 2014 presidential elections (Aras 2014). Therefore, depicting Gezi's impact on peripheral subjectivities in the film becomes a projection of political wishful thinking. In this respect, the narrative initiates a certain positionality between the center and the periphery, attributing a feminist sensibility to the center whose core aim is to transform gender relations and raise the consciousness of peripheral women. The film is critical of gendered forms of subordination in the periphery and highlights various issues. It is also important to note that the film does not represent peripheral women as passive victims, but as active agents who resist. However,

[3] For a commentary on #DirenKahkaha (Resist Laughter) activism, see Akyel (2014).

their means of resistance is problematic in the sense that it is imposed from above by the enlightening self of the center. In the end, *Mustang* does not provide the audience with the necessary narrative to comprehend the processes by which the sisters achieved their resistant characters.

2.2 Beyond Center–Periphery Dichotomy? Mutualities of Women's Experiences in *Tereddüt*

Can the Peripheral Woman Speak? An Intervention by Ustaoğlu

Tereddüt (*Clair Obscur*) [*Hesitation*] is the latest film by Yeşim Ustaoğlu, first screened at the 53rd Antalya International Film Festival on October 2016, winning Best Film, Best Director, and Best Actress awards (Vourlias 2016). Yeşim Ustaoğlu directed her first film in 1994 with *İz* [*The Trace*] and earned critical international acclaim with her further productions that include *Güneşe Yolculuk* [*Journey to the Sun*]—1999; *Bulutları Beklerken* [*Waiting for the Clouds*]—2003; *Pandora'nın Kutusu* [*Pandora's Box*]— 2008, which won the Golden Shell Award at San Sebastian International Film Festival; and *Araf* [*Somewhere in Between*]—2012. In her films, Ustaoğlu asks questions of womanhood (*Pandora's Box*, *Somewhere in Between*), migration and poverty (*Journey to the Sun*) and Turkish–Greek relations (*Waiting for the Clouds*), touching upon various issues dealing with gender relations and ethnic tensions in Turkey's present and past. The image of the periphery plays an important role in the director's narratives. Most of her main characters belong to peripheral identities, Kurds, Greeks and particularly individuals from the Black Sea region. This region was historically populated by Greeks until the foundation of the Turkish nation-state in the twentieth century and was later subject to population displacements due to the agreement between Turkey and Greece after the Turkish War of Independence (Shields 2013). Having lost its multiculturalism due to the attempts of nationalization throughout the Republican period, today the region is widely recognized as a conservative culture dominated by Islamism and Turkish nationalism. Moreover, the region's economic underdevelopment resulted in flows of migration to metropolitan areas such as Istanbul and Ankara from the 1960s onwards. As a result, the Black Sea region hosts an intersectionality of experiences along the lines of gender, class and ethnicity, which greatly influenced Ustaoğlu's film narratives.

In her previous film before *Tereddüt*, Ustaoğlu dealt with problematic gender relations in the periphery in *Araf*, which tells the story of a young woman, Zehra, living in Karabük province in the Black Sea region. Working at a gas station as a kitchen worker, Zehra meets Mahur, a truck driver who occasionally stops by the station. Zehra develops feelings for Mahur and the two end up having sex on a regular basis. From this point onwards, the film narrates Zehra's encounter with her sexuality, her attempt to pursue her sexual desires, to feel her body without really knowing it and the conflict she feels in dealing with an "illegitimate" sexual affair and concealing it. Eventually, Zehra ends up getting pregnant, Mahur leaves town and the following months pass with Zehra trying to hide the pregnancy from her family. Near the time of the birth, she makes an attempt to become sick and is taken to hospital, where she gives birth secretly in a toilet. In *Araf*, Ustaoğlu focuses on a common trauma that many women in conservative-peripheral cultural settings suffer: an unwanted child from an illegitimate relationship—criminal cases that create the stories of Turkish newspapers' crime reporting. In doing so, the film exposes the oppressive mechanisms of sexuality in the periphery through a female character who is deprived of any means to protect herself and discover, sufficiently learn about and confidently realize her sexuality, and hence experiences massive trauma. Such a female character is different from the women of *Mustang*. Unlike the young girls in *Mustang*—who are critical of the culture surrounding them; who attempt to fulfill their desires in a confident way despite prohibitions; who can know and learn about sexuality and other issues somehow—Zehra portrays the image of a peripheral woman who is besieged with repressive structures of a conservative ideology, which she cannot figure out how to escape. In this regard, the film's portrayal coincides with Gayatri Spivak's (1988) famous question, "Can the subaltern speak?"—interrogating the possibility of an active agency that can be performed by the individual in oppressed circumstances.

While it is clear that Zehra does not or cannot possess any agency to express or thwart her subordination, Ustaoğlu's *Tereddüt* hints at the possibility of a peripheral woman's recovering from trauma and speaking for herself, by means of the effort undertaken by another woman with higher cultural and economic capital. The film narrates the encounter of two women Elmas and Şehnaz in Kocaali, a coastal town in the Western Black Sea region. Elmas is a teenager married to a local man, while Şehnaz works as a psychiatrist in a state hospital doing mandatory service. Şehnaz is married to Cem, a successful and charismatic businessperson living in Istanbul. The opening scenes of the film introduce the lives of the two women. Elmas spends her entire time at home, not allowed to go out, carrying out housework and caring for her sick mother-in-law who lives next door. She is surrounded by oppressive mechanisms that do not allow her to have any private space; she is merely objectified as the servant in the family. She prepares and eats dinner at her mother-in-law's home once her husband arrives in the evening, and is obsessed with housework as she feels obliged to make everything perfect. Her only joy is to smoke on the balcony in secret when she has some free time, and watch the neighboring young girl who listens to music and dances most of the time. Elmas does not love her husband. Sex is traumatic for her and she prays that her husband does not want to have sex. However she is raped repeatedly by him and experiences a lot of pain during intercourse. The film initially points at patriarchal domination as an important element characterizing peripheral culture. Yet the narrative also highlights the diversity of women's experiences, especially with the dancing girl, and implies that not all women are victims of male domination. Women's experiences on the periphery may vary.

In the meantime, Şehnaz continues a long-distance relationship with Cem, chatting online in the evenings, where they fantasize about each other and Cem masturbates. On the weekends, Şehnaz returns to Istanbul to visit Cem and is shocked when she finds him watching porn by himself. Cem then approaches Şehnaz, tries to ease her frustration and the two end up having sex. At that point, it appears that Şehnaz wants to have sex, but she is not entirely happy with the situation. During her visit, Şehnaz and Cem hang out in Cem's business circles, consisting of high-cultured individuals dancing together the whole night, yet leaving Şehnaz alienated from everything happening around her, and in particular feeling distant from her relationship. Upon Şehnaz's arrival at Kocaali, tragic events unfold. That morning, Elmas is found at home on her balcony, pale and shivering. She is taken to hospital by the police for a medical examination. A male gynecologist, Umut, and Şehnaz examine Elmas, finding her arms and genitals bruised and injured. A police report shows that Elmas's husband has died in the night from carbon monoxide poisoning and Elmas is the prime suspect. Elmas's mother-in-law is also found dead, having overdosed on insulin, and the police suspect Elmas of murdering her since she is the one who normally looks after her. At this point, the film does not reveal the events of that night; we only see Elmas being raped by her husband and afterwards being ordered to add more wood to the fire. The film plays on the suspicion that Elmas may be the murderer. Ultimately, the suspense relies on Elmas' testimonial, which she continuously fails to give despite Şehnaz's efforts. Şehnaz, tries to calm Elmas down: "You lost your husband, mother," "You don't need to be afraid," "I am here to help you," "Tell me about yourself." But Elmas fails to respond. The first time Elmas answers Şehnaz is when Şehnaz asks "How many years have you been married?" Elmas responds, "Two." When Şehnaz then asks "What about your sex life?" Elmas gets angry saying, "Do not talk about this, it is a sin, it is a sin." Elmas is still far from giving a proper testimony.

Periphery as a Mutual Ground for Women's Subordination

The initial encounter between Şehnaz and Elmas constitutes a significant threshold in the narrative in terms of center–periphery relations. Şehnaz is an educated, cultured psychiatrist, who is knowledgeable and aware of sexuality and human behavior. The location of her mandatory service, Kocaali, is significant since it is a town located between the Black Sea and Marmara regions. At the west end of the Black Sea region, Kocaali is the closest town to Istanbul. Şehnaz is not fully resident in Kocaali, but travels back and forth to Istanbul on a weekly basis. At first, the periphery is only meaningful to Şehnaz as an obligatory step in her career, as it is for every medical doctor. However, her meeting with Elmas increases her engagement with the periphery, provides meaning to her life and causes her to question her relationship and social environment. As the narrative unfolds, Şehnaz gets increasingly alienated from her life in Istanbul. The film begins to portray two interrelated narratives of different women, focusing particularly on the acts of symbolic violence that Şehnaz experiences in her relationship. One important scene is where Şehnaz wakes up alone at night during a visit to Istanbul and finds Cem watching porn in the living room; she then approaches Cem to have sex with him. On this occasion, Şehnaz turns herself into a sex object, which brings about a self-realization that she can be a part of Cem's life as long as she is a sex object that accompanies Cem's sexual fantasies. Once intercourse has finished, Şehnaz continues to masturbate, signaling her disillusionment in her relationship. In this respect, the narrative exposes the mutuality of experiences that peripheral woman and privileged woman at the center share—that is, objectification through male sexual desire. Elmas and Şehnaz are two women who feel oppressed by the same problem, despite their different cultural and classed belongings.

Şehnaz's alienation from her relationship continues signified by Cem's insistence at drinking wine at dinner, even though Şehnaz prefers raki. In the meantime, Şehnaz befriends the gynecologist, Umut, who is from Kocaali. They wander along the coastline, sharing information and insights about Elmas's case and have long conversations where Şehnaz truly feels fulfilled. Contrary to the behavioral codes imposed on her in Istanbul, she drinks raki with Umut, whose name means "hope" in Turkish. Their developing relationship marks a crucial point in the narrative that highlights the empowering agency of the periphery over the center as it establishes the complicated relations of trauma and healing between the center and the periphery: Şehnaz is trying to heal Elmas while she is being healed by a man from the periphery, Umut. After spending an enjoyable evening in Umut's house, Şehnaz and Umut have sex, and Şehnaz experiences an orgasm. Having finally been sexually satisfied, Şehnaz now faces the problem of cheating on her husband, as her relationship continues to deteriorate. She lies to Cem about her not returning to Istanbul for the weekend and is undecided on how to deal with her relationship.

In the meantime, Şehnaz continues her efforts to encourage Elmas to give her testimony. They have two main sessions. In the first session, Elmas recalls the memory of when her mother forced her to drop out of school and to marry her husband. Şehnaz turns her process of narration into a role-playing game with objects, through which Elmas remembers the past. Yet her memory is so fragile and fragmented that the audience only gets glimpses of the story behind her oppression. Through their conversation we learn that Elmas was married at 13 and she is younger than the official age found on her identification documents. Her official age was increased after her father's application to court, where Elmas had to testify that she was older, afraid of being punished by her father if she refused. This fact would mean she would potentially receive a shorter prison sentence as she would be recognized as a child. Their second session takes place when Şehnaz asks Elmas about the night of the alleged murders. Elmas provides a fragmented account of what happened that night. She responds in a traumatized manner with a discontinuous narrative. "I was a parasite in that house, I prayed so that he wouldn't come, I do not remember, he held me with his claws. God please forgive me, God please forgive me." As Elmas fails to recall the event, the audience is left undecided about her guilt. Her not being able to remember could be considered as an act of resistance; perhaps she committed the crimes, but doesn't admit her guilt because she had no choice other than to murder the agents of her oppression. What distinguishes Elmas's character as a peripheral woman compared with the characters in *Mustang* is that Elmas is portrayed as a woman with a religious vocabulary who is veiled, signifying her religious personality. Contrary to the sisters in *Mustang*, whose representations are completely devoid of any Islamic signifiers, as if they were projected on the region from a Western society with a secularized imagery—which contradicts the religious culture dominating the villages in the Black Sea region— Elmas refers to her belief that she should bear the traumas that she encounters. The director's preference to designate her character as such reflects her insider position to the culture that she narrates through her film, strengthening the representation of the woman in the periphery by taking into consideration the role that religion plays in daily life.

The final scenes of the film include two distinct representations from the periphery and the center. On one hand, Elmas is trying to recover; although she is not back to full health mentally or physically, the narrative implies that she is making progress. We see her sitting with her friend, the dancing girl next door, who listens to music and gives one of her earphones to Elmas so that she too can listen. Elmas is still exhausted, but she doesn't refuse her offer and listens to the music. On the other hand, Şehnaz is in Istanbul having dinner with Cem in a disinterested manner. They have a huge quarrel about their relationship and Şehnaz accuses Cem of narcissism and lack of motivation in their relationship. Cem rejects the charges, defending himself but continues his oppressive behavior by not allowing Şehnaz to leave. Hours later, exhausted by fighting, Şehnaz leaves and drives away in tears. The film ends here. The final scene marks the transformation of a privileged, high-cultured, middle-class woman of the center in a seemingly perfect relationship into total disillusionment and disappointment, without exactly knowing how to find a solution. We do not know Şehnaz's decision about her future, or whether Elmas will testify or not; we are left with an unresolved dilemma between the center and the periphery, a state of hesitation that the film's name suggests.

This particular hesitation deconstructs the unified, enlightening, empowering female self of the center as conveyed by *Mustang*; Şehnaz's process of healing the peripheral woman turns out to be an exploration of her self-realization, fragmentation, hesitation and discontent in her life. Thus, although there is still a hierarchy between the different women in the center and the periphery, the narrative suggests that all women are oppressed by men regardless of their class and cultural belonging. Unlike *Mustang*, which proposes a narrative of enlightenment achieved by the sisters—by efforts of the center—and violently countered by the peripheral ideology, *Tereddüt* focuses on the mutualities of women's experiences and redefines the periphery as a cultural geography where such mutualities can manifest to address not only the problems of peripheral woman, but also of women of a higher class and cultural status. The periphery is not an oppressive setting that can be empowered and corrected by the center's ideological interpellation of the peripheral subject; it is rather a space that can be productive by means of mutualizing different women's experiences that would be helpful in exposing male-dominated culture. Elmas is deprived of the means to speak for herself since, as a woman experiencing the oppressing cultural mechanisms in the periphery, she does not have sufficient confidence or the means to express her personality. Yet this does not mean that she is a passive victim; her act of murder symbolizes a resistance attempt against her subordination. *Tereddüt* is a narrative that points out that the peripheral woman cannot speak (Elmas fails to testify); yet it also propounds that Şehnaz cannot speak. However, it shows that the women can share their traumas, uncover their problems and heal themselves by coming together, which brings forward the possibility of being able to speak. The periphery cannot speak without the help of the center, as the center cannot face its problems without its experience at the periphery; *Tereddüt* is a film of the mutuality of women's experiences through the interdependence of the center and the periphery.

2.3 The Demystification of the Center in *Yozgat Blues*

Yozgat Blues (2013) is the second film by director Mahmut Fazıl Coşkun after *Uzak İhtimal* [*Wrong Rosary*] of 2009. The film won the FIBRESCI prize in the 29th Warsaw International Film Festival, alongside Best Film, Best Director, Best Scenario and Best Actor awards at the Adana International Film Festival. The focus on the mutualities between the center and the periphery constitute a major discourse in Coşkun's film language. *Uzak İhtimal* is the story of a *müezzin*, a religious preacher living in a peripheral region, who is appointed to a mosque in Istanbul's Galata province. Here he meets Clara, a young Christian woman training to become a nun, and the two engage in a complicated relationship. *Uzak İhtimal* sheds light on the kinds of transformations and negotiations that take place in the characters' minds with regard to their different faiths and as a result of a loving relationship. Similarly, *Yozgat Blues* extends its intercultural attempt to the negotiations of meaning between the center, Istanbul, and the periphery, Yozgat—a province located in the Central Anatolian region. As an analysis of the film underscores, *Yozgat Blues* provides a unique account of center–periphery relations in terms of the representation of the cultural other, with its emphasis on the empowering effect of the periphery parallel to the deconstruction of the center; a narrative strategy that extends the kind of arguments manifested in *Tereddüt*.

The Center as an Experience of Cultural Alienation

The film begins with 58-year-old Yavuz singing Joe Dassin's famous song, "L'Été Indien" on the ground floor of a shopping mall in Istanbul. Originally a music teacher specializing in Western music, he lives alone having recently lost his father, and delivers music lessons to volunteers in courses organized by the municipality. He meets Neşe who attends one of his courses, and she asks him about the "Yozgat business" that Yavuz mentioned to her previously, regarding the offer that he received to perform his music in Yozgat. Neşe is looking for a job to make extra money as she is struggling to make a living working as a salesperson in a shopping mall. After a while Yavuz decides to accept the offer as a possible solution to his financial problems and they travel to Yozgat together to sing in a friend's lounge. They begin to perform Western music, mostly French romance–pop songs, which do not appeal to the majority of Yozgat residents due to cultural barriers and different tastes in music. Yet Yavuz is initially optimistic and he and Neşe give an interview to the *Yeni Yozgat* [*New Yozgat*] newspaper about their arrival in town, and acknowledge their "different" music style by telling the people of Yozgat that they make good music and expect everyone to listen to them in the lounge.

In the meantime, Yavuz and Neşe share two separate rooms in a hotel suite and begin a life together. As they spend time in town, Yavuz and Neşe begin to encounter the locals and form relationships. When he goes to his barber shop, Yavuz meets Sabri, a hairdresser who is a friend of Kamil who works in the local radio station hosting poetry shows. Yavuz and Neşe's meetings with locals intensifies the depth of the narrative of local lives. We hear the sound of an imam quoting the Quran to the public through the mosque speakers, indicating the religious aspects of daily life in a peripheral province. Additionally, we see Sabri having a haircut prior to meeting a young local woman—a potential wife—in a local café, under the supervision of their respective family members who are sitting a few tables behind them. A high-school graduate working in the dowry store in town, the woman is dressed in traditional clothes and is veiled, she seems happy with the prospect of a potential marriage with Sabri. She is surprised when Sabri tells her that he plans to open a women's hairdressing salon, although he currently works in a barber's shop. Sabri attends the gatherings of men in houses and listens to religious stories, indicating the kind of daily conversation of the locals. While Sabri is undecided about his marriage, he receives an offer from Yavuz to serve as his hairdresser before his performances. He starts the job and continues the relationship with his potential wife. This woman keeps asking Sabri questions about his decision to open a women's hairdressing salon, Sabri replies that he is trained as a women's hairdresser and this occupation will earn him good money. Furthermore, the woman asks, "Are you praying regularly?" Sabri replies, "Occasionally, but I do not miss Friday prayers."[4]

So far, the film highlights the central importance of religion in the daily lives of the locals in a peripheral town. However, the presence of religious discourse does not mean that every individual deems it significant in their lives. During his meetings with his potential wife, Sabri experiences a cultural examination based on gendered and religious questions. He resists the idea that men can only be employed as male hairdressers in a strictly gender-segregated peripheral town, and declares his ambition to open a women's hairdressing salon. Moreover, he doesn't have strict and intimate ties with his religious duties; he fulfills his performance of religiosity by simply showing up at Friday prayers as all men are obliged to do, without any further engagement. On the other hand, the woman occupies the position of an examiner, directing questions to Sabri about his tendency to resist conservative ideology, getting disillusioned with the responses that she receives. While the distance between the two grows, Sabri finds himself increasingly involved in Neşe's life. He offers her new hairstyles and they spend time together in town, socializing in cafés. In one of their meetings, they come across Kamil, who hosts shows in a local radio station, cites poetry and writes prose. Kamil is charmed to see Yavuz and

---

[4] Friday prayer is a religious obligation for men in Islam to visit the mosque on Fridays and pray in front of the imam regularly, in addition to their obligations to pray five times in a day. Sabri's quote implies that he is not practicing Islam regularly as obligated, but participates in Friday prayers as is expected by the community.

Neşe performing Western music in Yozgat, saying that "Yozgat is proud of you," and that all Yozgaters should listen to their music. Kamil invites Yavuz and Neşe to the radio station and further convinces Neşe to take part in his poetry-reading show at the municipality's performance hall. Kamil portrays an unusual character that one might associate with the periphery—a radio programmer who claims to be writing an autobiographical novel, defining himself as the "carrier of all the cultural works in Yozgat." His presence in the narrative shows that there are attempts at cultural production in the periphery and that the periphery is not totally devoid of aesthetic consciousness of the agents engaged in cultural work. Accordingly, as the representatives of different cultural environments, Yavuz and Kamil share a certain isolation from mainstream culture in the periphery dominated by conservative ideology. However, the difference is that Kamil possesses a certain name and title in Yozgat—the "radio, poetry guy"— whereas Yavuz increasingly feels himself as worthless, with no change in the situation he was experiencing back in Istanbul.

Yavuz's isolation reaches its peak when his friend and boss, Yaşar, terminates their agreement due to low revenues. Surprised with what he witnessed, Yavuz initially rejects the lack of interest in his music. "We are doing good music, all the press, radio ... People liked us ... it was going well." It appears that Yavuz's words are just wishful thinking and the people of Yozgat pay more attention to *Arabesk* or folk songs than Western popular music.[5] Considering the possible breakdown that Neşe may experience on hearing the news, Yavuz convinces Yaşar to allow them to continue performing without being paid. Picking up the habit of smoking due to his depression, he decides to sell his guitar to pay their hotel bills. He starts singing at wedding ceremonies to earn money, where he experiences a similar kind of audience that he experienced in Istanbul's shopping malls. He sings his French songs to the crowds, but nobody listens. Different from Dilek in *Mustang* and Şehnaz in *Tereddüt*, who spend time in the periphery as part of their mandatory service, Yavuz chooses to travel to Yozgat. The periphery is a location where he can earn a living, however he fails both in Istanbul and Yozgat. In this regard, the character of Yavuz and his experiences correspond to an argument regarding the failure and the paradox of Turkey's modernization project. As the representative of

---

[5] *Arabesk* is defined as the music of the peripheral populations migrating to metropolitan areas, representing the peripheral subject's disillusionment from and the failure to adapt to urban life. For detailed analysis on the phenomena, see Özbek (1991) and Stokes (1992).

Western culture, Yavuz's songs only serve as background music in Istanbul's shopping malls and at Yozgat wedding ceremonies. For Yavuz, there is no difference between the experience of a Western identity at the center and its manifestation in the periphery; the narrative does not secure a superior position for Yavuz during his encounter with the periphery as the cultural other. Yavuz himself is the cultural other, alienated from a culture, an economy and politics that claim to lean toward Western values, but merely uses it as make-up, an appearance to act as if it is pursuing such values. In this respect, the superior gaze of the characters arriving at the periphery in *Mustang* and *Tereddüt* is replaced by the ordinariness, insignificance and almost non-existence of an Istanbulite individual. Eventually, the character of Yavuz serves to demystify the subject located at the center, who others the peripheral individual with its superiority.

Peripheral Masculinities: A Deconstructive Attempt

As Yavuz travels through nothingness, Neşe's experience of the periphery progresses in a striking manner. As she befriends Sabri, they work together in opening his hairdressing salon for women. Concurrently, she works with Kamil by singing at his poetry recitals. Their relationship develops and Sabri asks Neşe to marry him. Neşe informs Yavuz that she has agreed to the marriage and Yavuz celebrates their decision. Neşe leaves their apartment, leaving Yavuz alone. A while later Yavuz decides to leave town and says goodbye to Neşe and Sabri. The final scene of the movie shows him sitting alone at the bus station waiting for a bus back to Istanbul. The experience of the periphery devastates Yavuz as he has not achieved anything. By contrast, Neşe gains her self-confidence and establishes herself as a worthy individual in the periphery. As a woman disappearing among the large crowds of the metropolitan area with an ordinary occupation, she becomes empowered in the periphery and starts her life over. Among women in *Mustang*, *Tereddüt* and *Yozgat Blues*, Neşe is the only character whose life is positively transformed by her interactions in the periphery.

Yozgat Blues also critically assesses the boundaries of peripheral masculinities by not offering a clear narrative of male domination and associating its male characters with men benefiting from the patriarchal dividend. On the contrary, Sabri and Kamil are characters who engage in equal relationships with Neşe without objectifying or oppressing her. Sabri even contributes to the ways in which Neşe can feel more beautiful by styling her hair. In a similar vein, Kamil integrates Neşe's talents and her passion for music into his poetry project, without imposing an ideological agenda on her. Therefore, the peripheral men in *Yozgat Blues* are not represented as the perpetrators of patriarchal subordination, but as men actualizing behaviors that stand outside the boundaries of hegemonic masculinities, which may be a factor that allows Neşe to be fulfilled as a self-confident woman. In summary, *Yozgat Blues* offers a dynamic and unexpected narrative regarding the center–periphery conflict that scrutinizes the representations of the unified self, associated with either the center or the periphery, by seeking to demystify the relationships and hierarchies perceived between two different cultural and geographical locations.

2.4 Conclusion

This chapter argues that the center–periphery dichotomy is a crucial strategy in contemporary Turkish cinema employed by different directors to imagine the cultural other from a gendered perspective. The discussion of Deniz Gamze Ergüven's *Mustang*, Yeşim Ustaoğlu's *Tereddüt* and Mahmut Fazıl Coşkun's *Yozgat Blues* shows that there are significant differences regarding the ways in which the films approach the issues of cultural difference. In *Mustang*, the periphery is represented as the bearer of a conservative, patriarchal ideology that has close ties with the country's hegemonic political discourses. As a response to gendered forms of domination, *Mustang* proposes the libertarian values possessed by the feminist consciousness of the central agent, who can raise the consciousness of peripheral women, empower them as free individuals to pursue their desires and ambitions. In *Tereddüt*, the relations between the center and the periphery are represented through mutualities of different women's experiences, rather than clear-cut hierarchies between them. The encounter of women belonging to different cultures and classes results in creating the problem of "who is healing or empowering whom" as women's identities get increasingly fragmented, thus critically negotiating the perceived boundaries between the center and the periphery with a focus on women's common struggle against male domination in society. Lastly, *Yozgat Blues* offers an alternative account regarding the center–periphery conflict, where the narrative tends to demystify the superiority of the center by noticing the multiplicity of experiences that the periphery entails as well as drawing attention to the possibilities of empowerment that the periphery can offer.

Bibliography

Açar, M. (2015, October 23). Bir Özgürlük Çığlığı [A Cry of Freedom]. Retrieved from http://www.haberturk.com/yazarlar/mehmet-acar/1143761-bir-ozgurluk-cigligi

Akyel, E. (2014). #Direnkahkaha (Resist Laughter): "Laughter Is a Revolutionary Action". *Feminist Media Studies, 14*(6), 1093–1094.

Aras, U. (2014, August 11). Erdogan Wins Turkey's Presidential Election. Retrieved from http://www.aljazeera.com/news/middleeast/2014/08/erdogan-wins-turkey-presidential-election-2014810172347586150.html

Dorsay, A. (2015, October 23). Görkemli bir kadın filmi, bir çağdaş sinema başyapıtı [A Magnificent Woman Film, a Contemporary Cinema Masterpiece]. Retrieved from http://t24.com.tr/yazarlar/atilla-dorsay/gorkemli-bir-kadin-filmi-bir-cagdas-sinema-basyapiti,13009

Jones, E. (2016, May 12). Mustang Movie Channels Female 'Power'. Retrieved from http://www.bbc.com/news/entertainment-arts-36225698

Kural, N. (2015, October 24). Evrensele ulaştı ama yerele hitap edecek mi? [It Reached the Universal But Will It Access the Local?]. Retrieved from http://www.milliyet.com.tr/evrensele-ulasti-ama-yerele-hitap/nil-kural/cumartesi/yazardetay/24.10.2015/2136866/default.htm

Özbek, M. (1991). Popüler kültür ve Orhan Gencebay arabeski [Popular Culture and the Arabesk of Orhan Gencebay]. Istanbul: İletişim Yayınları.

Shields, S. (2013). The Greek-Turkish Population Exchange: Internationally Administered Ethnic Cleansing. *Middle East Report, 43*(267), 2–6.

Spivak, G. C. (1988). 'Can the Subaltern Speak?': Revised Edition, from the 'History' Chapter of Critique of Postcolonial Reason. In R. C. Morris (Ed.), *Can the Subaltern Speak? Reflections on the History of an Idea* (pp. 21–78). New York: Columbia University Press.

Stokes, M. (1992). *The Arabesk Debate: Music and Musicians in Modern Turkey.* Oxford: Clarendon Press.

Tuncer, A. Ö. (2016, February 8). Mustang bir Özgürleşme Filmi mi? [Is Mustang an Emancipation Film?]. Retrieved from http://www.5harfliler.com/mustang-bir-ozgurlesme-film-mi/

Vardan, U. (2015, October 24). Genel resim doğru ama… [The General Picture Is Correct However…]. Retrieved from http://www.hurriyet.com.tr/yazarlar/ugur-vardan/genel-resim-dogru-ama-40005458

Vourlias, C. (2016, October 23). Yeşim Ustaoğlu's 'Clair-Obscur' Wins Top Honors at Antalya Film Festival. Retrieved from http://variety.com/2016/film/global/antalya-film-festival-closing-ceremony-clair-obscur-1201898268/

Žižek, S. (2001). *Enjoy Your Symptom!: Jacques Lacan in Hollywood and Out.* New York: Routledge.

CHAPTER 3

The Making of a Militarized Self and the Other in Television Series: A Reformulation of the Center?

Abstract This chapter provides an analysis of three television series that were produced in Turkey in 2017: *Söz* [*The Promise*], *İsimsizler* [*The Nameless*] and *Savaşçı* [*The Warrior*]. These series are significant since they reflect the ongoing political and social tensions in Turkey with regard to the Kurdish issue. The narratives point out the making of a militarized, national self located at the center, which targets the figure of the enemy aiming to capture the periphery. In this regard, the periphery is discursively established as a battleground that needs to be controlled by the center, so that the militarized, national self can realize its potential. Within this representation, the narratives do not look at the kinds of social and cultural exclusion that the Kurdish community may suffer due to Turkey's long-running Kurdish issue. On the contrary, Kurdish civilians are generally portrayed as the state's loyal citizens, content with the center's policies. It is important to note that these series are produced by television channels whose televisual discourses, particularly soap operas, show the lifestyles of secular Turks, rather than Turkish society's religious or Islamic elements. This chapter discusses the ways in which secular Turks tend to secure themselves a privileged space at the center in addition to the social segments represented by the government by means of signifying the periphery in a militarized manner.

Keywords Militarism • Television • TV series • Kurdish issue • Kemalism • Nationalism

© The Author(s) 2018
A. Nas, *Media Representations of the Cultural Other in Turkey*,
https://doi.org/10.1007/978-3-319-78346-8_3

3.1 Periphery as a National Problem

Turkey's Kurdish issue dates back to the early Republican era when the nation-state was established according to a single, homogeneous Turkish national identity, facilitating the structural exclusion of Kurdish populations in terms of their linguistic and cultural rights (Gunter 2008; Heper 2007). After decades of dispute, the emergence of the PKK (Kurdistan Workers' Party) in 1984 transformed the conflicts into an armed struggle. The 1990s witnessed the growing visibility of Kurdish politics with the formation of several political parties, many of which have been considered the representatives of "terrorism" and "separatism" and were banned by the Constitutional Court between 1990 and 2009.[1] What characterized this era was the silencing of politics in dealing with the issue as the state prioritized military struggle over a democratic solution. From the early Republican period up to the 2000s, the Kurdish periphery was formulated as a national problem, which the center needed to counter militaristically so that national sovereignty could be strengthened.

The JDP's rise to power in 2002 changed various dynamics in the state's views on the Kurdish issue. Positioning itself as the representative of the periphery, the government's initial step was to lift the state of emergency in the Turkish south-eastern region populated by Kurdish people, which had lasted for 15 years.[2] The government's efforts focused on the promotion of the Kurdish issue and getting it on the political agenda, particularly with the "Democratic Initiative Process" or the "Kurdish Opening" that took off in 2009 (Kardaş and Balci 2016, p. 155). The primary aim of the process was to open up a space for a democratic discussion of the Kurdish issue, accompanied by negotiations with Kurdish representatives. Despite various positive attempts regarding a democratic solution to the Kurdish issue, relations between the two parties were greatly damaged after the general election held on June 7, 2015, which ended up with the JDP losing its majority in parliament and unable to form a single-party government (Kardaş and Balci 2016, p. 159).

---

[1] "Factbox: Turkey's history of banning parties" May 3, 2010. Reuters. Available: https://www.reuters.com/article/us-turkey-constitution-banned-factbox/factbox-turkeys-history-of-banning-parties-idUSTRE6423UA20100503, accessed: December 20, 2017.

[2] "Avrupa Konseyi Olağanüstü Hal'in Kalkmasından Memnuniyet Duyduğunu Bildirdi" ["European Council told that it was pleased to see the state of emergency lifted"]. December 12, 2002. Anadolu Ajansı. Available: https://www.ab.gov.tr/_21313.html, accessed: December 12, 2017.

Meanwhile, the pro-Kurdish People's Democratic Party (PDP) managed to pass the 10% threshold, winning 13.1% of the vote and holding 80 seats in parliament, which was an important moment for Kurdish politics.

During the negotiations to form a coalition government, there was a sudden breakdown of peace negotiations following the PKK's declaration to forge an armed struggle in July 2015. The elections were repeated in November 2015, which ended up with the JDP regaining enough seats to form a single-party government. This period also witnessed the PKK's attempts to capture cities and form independent governorships, which was met with the government declaring a state of emergency in the region. Turkey was also targeted by ISIS terror attacks in this period. Between July 2015 and January 2017, 596 civilians, 580 soldiers and 311 police lost their lives as a result of terror attacks in metropolitan areas and violent conflicts in the region.[3] In this period, the government's discourse on the Kurdish issue was largely transformed; the democratic initiative process was cancelled and Erdoğan repeatedly declared that, "There is no Kurdish issue, but a terrorism issue."[4] All these events led to a government vision on "the war on terror," which was disseminated to the public mostly via news covering the "martyrdom of soldiers," sacrificing their lives for the unity of the nation. Eventually, these processes revitalized nationalism by the legitimization of militarist discourses and indicated a departure from a democratic solution to the issue, similar to the situation observed in the 1990s.

The "military" television series, *The Promise* on Star TV, *The Nameless* on Kanal D and *The Warrior* on FOX TV can be considered as the reflections of recent political events on the televisual discourse, and a comment on the media representations of the self and the other. In this regard, these series employ narrative strategies that illustrate the ways in which the periphery is represented as a problem to be dealt with to ensure and strengthen a Turkish national self-identity located at society's center. Anthropologist Tayfun Atay acknowledges that these series can be considered as "bribes" given by media outlets to the government after the April 2017 constitutional referendum, where Erdoğan's proposal for presidential

---

[3] "Terör Bilançosu" ["The Outcome of Terror"]. May 11, 2017. Diken. Available: http://www.diken.com.tr/teror-bilancosu-7-haziran-2015ten-bu-yana-596-sivil-580-asker-311-polis-hayatini-kaybetti/, accessed: December 12, 2017.
[4] "There's no Kurdish issue in Turkey, just terrorism: Erdoğan" January 6. 2016. *Hürriyet Daily News*. Available: http://www.hurriyetdailynews.com/theres-no-kurdish-issue-in-turkey-just-terrorism-Erdoğan-93511, accessed December 12, 2017.

system won by securing 51.4% of the vote.[5] While I agree that these series may reflect attempts by secularist television channels to maintain good relations with the government, I prefer to set out an alternative view by arguing that the distinct televisual discourse put forward by these series indicates a resurgence of secular Turks who wish to re-establish themselves at the center by negotiating their boundaries with the periphery.

3.2 Orientalizing the Periphery, Fulfilling the Self: *The Promise* of Revenge

The series *The Promise* was aired on television on April 3, 2017, and narrates the story of a group of soldiers forming a special forces team to combat terrorists in Turkey's south-eastern provinces. *The Promise* has proved itself to be one of the most successful productions of Star TV. As of December 2017, the series has 1.2 million subscribers on its official YouTube channel, 1.5 million followers on Instagram and 250 thousand followers on Facebook.[6] The series won Best Director, Best Actor and Best Series Music awards in the Pantene Golden Butterfly Television Awards in December 2017.[7] Inspired by the series, a mobile game was produced in December 2017 where users could select one of the characters, lead a military squad and undertake operations against the enemy.[8] Furthermore, the series was officially supported by the General Staff of the Republic of Turkey and Ministry of National Defense.[9] The actors went through intensive military training for two months, led by former special

---

[5] Atay provided analyses of the series in his daily columns in *Cumhuriyet* newspaper. See Atay (2017a, b, c).

[6] Söz official YouTube page: https://www.youtube.com/channel/UCJkBcPylctTT0_jVC5XMFIg/; Söz official Instagram page: https://www.instagram.com/sozdizi/?hl=en/; Söz official Facebook page: https://www.facebook.com/sozdizi/

[7] "Winners of the 44th Golden Butterfly Awards." Available: https://www.turkishcelebritynews.com/winners-of-the-44th-golden-butterfly-awards-2017.html

[8] "Söz—Oyun" ["The Promise—The Game"]. Available: https://www.youtube.com/watch?v=B5V0LinKiak

[9] "'Söz' dizisinden 5 dakikalık özel bölüm" [5-minutes special episode from The Promise]. April 2, 2017. NTV. Available: https://www.ntv.com.tr/yasam/soz-dizisinden-5-dakikalik-ozel-bolum,BinYhvejNk2mlIGVzAeUkg, accessed: December 12, 2017.

forces units.[10] *The Promise* produced a perfect simulation of the viewers' experience of traumatic events in Turkey's recent history by facilitating particular dynamics of cultural representation in terms of center–periphery distinctions.

Imagining the Peaceful Co-Existence with the Cultural Other

The first episode of *The Promise* begins with two significant scenes of martyrdom, which reflects the traumatic experiences that the Turkish national self went through in recent years. The opening sequences of the series show a member of the special forces, Selo, dying after an attack in a mountain setting. As his fellow soldiers commemorate his death, the news is given to his relatives who are devastated. Selo's wife, family and relatives burst into tears once they hear about the incident. They hang the Turkish flag from the balconies of their homes, simultaneously displaying sadness and determination. In the meantime, a narrator comments on the course of events, telling how Selo's relatives are proud of giving their son to God as a martyr; how his father does not cry indicating that they will not lose against the enemy; and how the whole neighborhood decorates every building with Turkish flags to signify its pride in martyrdom. The opening scenes give the audience an overview of the kind of psychological trauma that the audience themselves have been experiencing with the recent loss of hundreds of soldiers' lives. Yet it is also the primary narrative strategy that establishes the essential motive of the series, the imagining of a nation by the embodiment of the national self through death during the struggle against the enemy.

The enemy gains visibility as the narrative progresses in the second scene of the first episode where a terror attack takes place in a shopping mall. The protagonist, Yavuz, is a professional soldier serving as a lieutenant in the army. A handsome man with a perfect body, he represents the superior masculine self at the center. He has proposed marriage to his girlfriend, Merve, who is based in Istanbul. Merve gave up her career in Europe after meeting Yavuz, sacrificing her career for love. She is fre-

[10] "'Söz' dizisi oyuncuları askeri eğitim aldı" ["The actors in *The Promise* received military training"]. March 24, 2017. NTV. Available: https://www.ntv.com.tr/galeri/yasam/soz-dizisi-oyuncuları-askeri-egitim-aldi,RsgIKGN0vEyYX8YNE4H7lg/b9y9gHE9gUablzSKx-sQUdg, accessed: December 12, 2017.

quently alone as Yavuz is often away on military operations. When Merve accepts Yavuz's marriage proposal, they go to a mall to celebrate over dinner. In the mall, Yavuz sees several men acting suspiciously and tells Merve to leave the area while he takes action. Feeling certain that the men are preparing for a terror attack, Yavuz follows them and begins to shoot when he sees them taking out their rifles. However, he is unable to prevent a suicide bomber from detonating her bomb. In the meantime, Merve tries to save a defenseless child caught up in the shooting, but ends up being badly injured by the suicide bomber and hospitalized. There are dozens of civilian loses before Yavuz manages to kill some of the terrorists, thus saving the lives of hundreds of other civilians.

In the scenes that follow, Yavuz waits for positive news about Merve. Unfortunately she dies. Her funeral ceremony is that of a martyr and Yavuz takes an oath to take revenge on her killers. His commander, Erdem, urges him "not to seek revenge since he is a professional soldier and he cannot mourn," defining the boundaries of a militarized subjectivity. However, on the way to the airport, Yavuz hears on the news that one of the terrorists who managed to escape has taken a pregnant woman hostage. Yavuz travels to the hostage setting and manages to save the woman by neutralizing the terrorist. The initial sequences of *The Promise* establish a clear-cut hierarchy between the militarized national self located at the center and the figure of the terrorist who is ruthless and aims to harm the center. The narrative implicitly states that the terrorists target the strength and the peace of the nation, with a definite victimization of the national self. In this regard, the series initiates a narrative on the center through the terrorist figure; the scenes show that Merve, Yavuz, Erdem and their families are middle-class secular Turks. In this regard, the series facilitates an initial position where the center represented by secular Turks is victimized by the terrorist figure.

The emphasis on victimization is further narrated in a symbolic scene that takes place in Mardin, the army headquarters and a historic city in Turkey's eastern provinces with its ethnically diverse population consisting of Kurds and Arabs. Based in the military headquarters, Erdem is living in Mardin, and his wife and daughter, Nazlı, frequently visit him from Istanbul. Nazlı and her mother visit the historic bazaar of Mardin's old town before their departure for Istanbul. The scene is a significant manifestation of an encounter between the center and the periphery; the periphery is an exotic object of curiosity for Nazlı and her mother who observe the Orient as tourists. Nazlı enters a store of musical instruments where an elderly man is playing a *saz*, a traditional stringed instrument in Turkish and Kurdish cultures. The man sings in Turkish and Nazlı is fascinated by the music, then decides to accompany the traditional folk song by playing a violin. Once the song ends, the elderly man and Nazlı have a conversation and Nazlı tells him she is studying music in the state conservatory in Istanbul. The scene is a perfect illustration of the peaceful co-existence of the East and the West, the center and the periphery as the center imagines it. The center is portrayed as the modern, Westernized national self, which peacefully co-exists with the peripheral other who is mysterious and exotic, reproducing a self-Orientalist formula. Furthermore, the peripheral agent is not portrayed in a multi-cultural stance; he is speaking and singing in Turkish, where others might be speaking in Kurdish or in Arabic in the region. The narrative imagines that there are no problems that the peripheral other faces in this relationship, particularly due to cultural or linguistic rights. Strikingly, once Nazlı leaves the store, she is kidnapped by terrorists; the terrorist figure interrupts the harmonious existence of the center and the periphery. At this point, a masculinist narrative asserts its influence as one of the primary strategies in the making of the Turkish national self. The conflict between the national self and a terrorist figure is reproduced through the victimization of women: Yavuz's lover is killed by a terrorist and Erdem's daughter is kidnapped. In turn, men tend to operate to save women and the nation altogether, showing a masculine superiority embodying the militarized national self represented by the center.

Periphery as a Battleground for the Center's Self-Fulfillment

The terror attack and the kidnapping crisis that imprint the core axis of the narrative revitalizes masculine superiority in the periphery through the formation of a collective unit that would perform that superiority, a team of special forces. As Erdem plans the operation to save his daughter, the terrorists publish a video demanding the release of their imprisoned fellows by the state in exchange for Nazlı, threatening to kill her if their demands are not met. The upper house of commanders orders Erdem to form a special forces team that would operate secretly to locate the terrorists. In the meantime, one of the commanders states that, "The terrorists should understand one thing, the state does not negotiate with the terrorists no matter what." The remark is crucial since it signifies a sharp transformation in the governmental discourse from peace negotiation processes to the military operations in recent years.

For his special forces team, Erdem recruits former soldiers living in Istanbul who show unconditional obedience. At this juncture, the narrative focuses on the stories of these soldiers and their determination to take the enemy. One of these soldiers, Mücahit, is defined as "insane," and is famous for saying, "Please God let me become a martyr." Mücahit's great grandfather died in World War I, his grandfather in the Cyrpus War in 1973 and his father in 2009 as a result of a terror attack while he was working as a police officer. Representing a generation of martyrs, Mücahit is seen in a flashback catching a terrorist in the mountains, beating him and insulting him. Mücahit complains that the terrorists are stupid, they are easily caught and that he will be denied the chance to become a martyr because of the stupidity of these enemies. In the persona of Mücahit, the special forces team represents the militarized masculine self located at the center, which has a duty to eliminate the threats in the periphery so that the center and the periphery can co-exist peacefully. The depth of the characters is the main reason why *The Promise* also produced a mobile phone game where users can identify with these characters and wage a war against the enemy figure.

As the periphery is constituted as a battleground, the peripheral agent is represented in a rather ambiguous way. The Kurdishness of the locals is only implied rather than openly stressed. There is no mention of their potential problems with regard to their linguistic and cultural rights, the crucial factors that historically led to the development of the Kurdish issue. However, the peripheral other is not positioned as the enemy of the state either. Rather, they are portrayed as individuals who are oppressed by the terrorists. While the special forces team works on its plan to save Nazlı, a team member receives intelligence from a local boy, who shows them the location of the terrorists holding Nazlı hostage. Once the team reaches the house, the soldiers see that the terrorists have already departed and find the deceased body of the boy punished by the terrorists. This scene affirms the recent state discourse on the Kurdish issue, namely that there is not a Kurdish problem but a terrorism problem, as evident in the murder of an innocent Kurdish boy. The peripheral other is portrayed as someone who is oppressed by the terrorist and awaiting to be saved by the center.

The terrorists gather in another place to broadcast Nazlı's execution online. Yavuz finds them and saves Nazlı after an armed struggle. During his rescue attempt, Yavuz confronts the leader of the terrorists, Köse (who ordered the terror attack in Istanbul), and chokes him to death using the flag of the terrorist organization. The final scenes of the episode show Nazlı hugging her mother as the narrator says, "Everything is worth it just for this scene, soldiers die so that mothers can hug their children, babies can be born, our flag can freely float in the air and everyday new soldiers can be born." In the end, Erdem appoints Yavuz as the leader of the special forces team so that they can track down another terrorist—Çolak, a relative of Köse, seeking his revenge and planning to target civilian planes. In the meantime, Bahar, the daughter of a wealthy family in Istanbul and an ambitious medical doctor who tried to save Merve's life, visits Yavuz as she has developed feelings for him. Soon Bahar becomes a target for Çolak.

As the cultural other, the periphery in *The Promise* hosts the hegemonic struggle between the Turkish national self-identity represented by the center and the absolute perpetrator figure of the terrorist. The peripheral agent is totally devoid of ethnic identity, it is as if he/she is assimilated into the general Turkish culture and is satisfied with it. Culturally constituted by secular Turks, the center aims to save the periphery from the atrocities committed by terrorists in order to forge a coherent, national identity. Militarization is a key component of the formation of this national self. In the meantime, women appear as victims targeted by terrorists as the power struggle between two parties proceeds through the capturing and the saving of women in an objectified manner. The narrative also conveys the feeling that although the central subject's lifestyle is modern and Western, it is through the periphery that the center can fulfill its potential and regain its power. Merve, Bahar, Yavuz and Erdem are characters who are based in the center as Turks living secular lives, yet they give up their lives and careers at the center and move to the periphery to fulfill their national identity.

3.3 *The Nameless*: The Forming of a National Coalition at the Center

The first episode of *The Nameless* was aired on March 27, 2017, by Kanal D. The channel was owned by Doğan Holding before it was sold to Demirören Group in March 2018. Doğan's primary media discourse situated it as the representative of secularist Turks, with the *Hürriyet* newspaper's slogan being "Turkey belongs to Turks." The series began with high ratings and competed with its rivals, *The Promise* and *The Warrior*, during its first season; however, its second season failed as the series was cancelled after its 27th episode on December 16, 2017. Though not regarded as successful as *The Promise*, the series managed to reach a significant audience after March 2017, maintaining 200,000 followers on Facebook and 150,000 followers on Instagram.[11]

Revitalization of the National Self

The first episode of *The Nameless* begins by signaling that it narrates "real events in the course of struggle for the nation," dedicating the production to Muhammet Fatih Safitürk, the governor of Mardin's Derik province who was killed by the PKK in his governorship building on November 10, 2016. The first episode narrates this event, where terrorists bomb the governor's office. The governor dies in the bombing, but his son, who is playing next door, survives and experiences intense trauma that will follow him for the rest of his life. This event is the setting for the center's victimization in the periphery targeted by terrorists. The governor's murder provides the significant event in the narrative after which the center forms a team to regain its strength and encounter the enemy. As an ambitious bureaucrat, Fatih gives up on his career plans to move to Switzerland for further education and decides to replace the deceased governor voluntarily. The city is called "Virankaya," an imaginary setting symbolizing a Kurdish-populated province on Turkey's Iraqi border. Fatih considers Virankaya as a crucial setting that the terrorists aim to capture so that they can proceed further and declare independence from Turkey, uniting their Syrian and Iraqi borders. As Fatih undertakes his journey, he begins to assess the political situation and gather his team to counter the upcoming challenges.

At this point in the narrative, two crucial signifiers constitute the main discursive tools with which the series imagines the political complexities and power relations at the periphery. Firstly, the episode is designated with illustrations of several political agents that are clearly enemy figures. In doing so, the narrative claims to be inspired by real events, which indicates that the kinds of representations in the series offer the audience a certain way of comprehending recent events. According to the dominant view in the series, the PKK, referred to as *örgüt* [the organization], is supported

---

[11] İsimsizler official Facebook page is available at https://www.facebook.com/Isimsizler/; İsimsizler official Instagram page is available at https://www.instagram.com/isimsizler/?hl=en

by Western countries, namely, the "crusaders," who aim to speed up the decline of the Turkish nation-state to benefit their own interests in the region. The *örgüt* aims to unite its lands in northern Syria with Turkey's south-eastern provinces, where Virankaya occupies a critical position. The "West," as governor Fatih calls it, has declared its open support for the *örgüt* so that it can invade the cities and declare independence. The narrative shows that a Western-based non-governmental organization, which is claiming to be working on human rights in the region, is actually providing technical infrastructure and logistics to terrorists, since the bomb that murdered the governor was produced in its facilities. In addition, its members are frequently visiting *örgüt* bases in Syria to plot against Turkey and discuss strategies. On the other hand, there are forces within the Turkish nation-state, which secretly ally with Western ambitions and the *örgüt*'s progress, called "cryptos," that conceal themselves in state institutions. Formulating the enemy within and beyond the country's boundaries and providing the audience with a certain reading of recent events, the episode shows Fatih setting up a team to actively counter plans plotted against the country.

At this point, the second crucial signifier is integrated into the narrative regarding the facilitation of the special forces team. Fatih approaches many former soldiers who would devote themselves to the struggle. In doing so he meets two controversial figures, Dayı (the uncle) and former Lieutenant Olcay. Dayı is a middle-aged man with a Turkish nationalist identity. On the other hand, Olcay is an ex-soldier who was expelled from the army in the late 2000s. At this point, though not openly stressed, the narrative implies that Olcay is a victim of unfair trials conducted by prosecutors and soldiers affiliated to Fetullah Gülen, a self-exiled cleric residing in the USA accused of perpetrating the July 15, 2016 coup attempt. Once Fatih calls him for duty, Olcay shows his anger regarding past events, saying that "they were set up by traitors who abused the state institutions," and that they have a nation that needs to be saved from them. The gathering of Dayı and Olcay led by Fatih signals the formation of a national coalition against the terrorists and their allies. Hence the formation of a national coalition signals the revitalization of the national self located at the center through its struggle in the periphery as the locus of national sovereignty. Despite Fatih operating as the government's representative, this particular self is not an Islamized or a religious self; it is the extension of a secular Turkish self as seen by the major signifiers in terms of the lifestyles of Fatih's, Dayı's and Olcay's families. As a result, the national self is formed as a secularist establishment, devoid of any religious indicators that would signify Islamism and its way of life.

Hierarchizing the Peripheral Other in Relation to the Center

As the national coalition of forces has been formed, the narrative illustrates the ways in which the periphery is colonized by the enemy in various ways. The city mayor of Virankaya is a member of a Kurdish political organization—implying the PDP. The party is portrayed as defunct in terms of its political activities and services to the public. Its trucks are being used by *örgüt* to move weapons freely but discreetly. The mayor is frequently visited by *örgüt* members who give orders about their future actions toward their project of declaring independence. In one remarkable scene, the mayor tells an *örgüt* member that she won the election with 90% of the vote, and that they need not be in a hurry to declare independence since they already have the majority of public support. In response, the *örgüt* member threatens her by telling her that it is because of their support that she won the election, treating the mayor as a worthless politician. Due to the tense dynamics between the party and the *örgüt*, the mayor cannot work effectively and bring services to the public. The mayor is active in terms of political discourses, setting up public centers for youth to train them in tactics for disobedience against the state. Furthermore, the party's members of parliament use their political immunity to transport wanted terrorists from one place to another without being searched by the police. The narrative underscores that the primary role of legitimate Kurdish politics has been to support the *örgüt*. The periphery is colonized by the organization, and despite a few weak objections held by the party officers, Kurdish politics is deprived of the power to be a dominant force in the region. Therefore, the narrative highlights that what needs to be done is eliminate the dominance of the terrorists, who colonize not only the region but also the minds of the peripheral subjects.

In *The Nameless*, we see representations of the peripheral subject in a fragmented way. On the one hand, the peripheral individual is mostly portrayed as loyal to the state. Several characters that appear in the first episode establish the locals' perceptions of the state, revealing the ways in which the center imagines how the periphery imagines itself. In this regard, the locals complain about the party, accusing it of not providing services to the public and instead focusing on other business with *örgüt*.

Meanwhile, central government is appreciated for its investment in the region, in the construction of roads and other facilities that increase public wealth. The figure of the governor is perceived as an outsider who has close relations with peripheral subjects, asking them what their needs are and endeavoring to meet them. The locals contend that the reason why the previous governor was murdered was because of his services to the public and that terrorists will not allow the locals and government officers to form positive, long-lasting relationships. In a similar way, Fatih succeeds the deceased governor as the representative of the center who does not engage in a hierarchical relationship with the peripheral other by asserting power, but by servicing it in any way it needs. Despite the emphasis on services and raising the welfare of the periphery, there is no mention of any potential problems that Kurdish people may experience in terms of linguistic and cultural belonging. From this perspective, the peripheral subject is de-politicized and devoid of any rights claims due to a Kurdish identity or the long-lasting Kurdish issue. The narrative represents them as satisfied with their lives particularly due to the services granted by the government in terms of urban infrastructure.

In addition to the portrayal of peripheral other as obedient subjects of the state, the narrative also points at the fragmented subjectivities in the periphery by partially delving into the life of the terrorist figure. As the narrative acknowledges, 90% of residents voted for the pro-Kurdish party, and it is highly probable that the residents supporting the state under all conditions constituted the other 10% of the total population. This shows that there is a serious problem that the governor needs to deal with; as upon his arrival to town, Fatih visits the house of a governorship worker who has been injured in the bombing of the governor's office. The worker perfectly illustrates the peripheral subject obedient to the state as he hangs a Turkish flag on the walls of his home. However, he has a disobedient son. The child protests the governor's visit to the house by telling him that, "Our comrades are struggling for our pride." Fatih responds to him in a kind manner, telling him that they are brothers and sisters, that Kurds and Turks are friends and that together they fought against the enemy in the National War of Independence after World War I. The boy responds by saying, "I am fed up with Republic of Turkey's words." This is met with a harsh reaction from his father and the boy subsequently leaves the house. Fatih is not happy with how the father deals with the boy and urges him to treat his son nicely or the boy will continue to co-operate with the terrorists.

At this juncture, the mayor represents the Turkish national self who intends to "rehabilitate" the peripheral other that has been poisoned by the terrorists. Despite the attempt by the governor to communicate with the peripheral other oriented with radical and critical discourses regarding the state, it becomes hardly possible to hear the voice of the Kurdish individual regarding the sources of his oppression. In this respect, the way that the peripheral other is portrayed as a child signifies two layers of meaning. Firstly, the child cannot adequately represent himself and the people's demands, thus it becomes impossible for the audience to be exposed to alternative perceptions of a Kurdish reality. Secondly, the way in which Fatih treats the child signifies a particular hierarchy in the cultural other, where adult *örgüt* members are the absolute perpetrators, the Kurdish politicians come next who are not in charge of affairs but give weak objections, the child figure who is deceived by the terrorists but still can be saved and, finally, the local Kurdish people who are the loyal citizens of the state.

The Nameless is a narrative that affirms the state discourse and reminds the audience that there is no Kurdish issue in terms of the people of the region demanding certain rights, but there is the problem of terrorism. Terrorism is set up by the enemies of the state including internal and external groups. In this regard, an anti-Western sentiment is strongly established as a source of national awareness. Similar to *The Promise*, the first episode of *The Nameless* also ends with a martyrdom scene, where a young police officer dies as a result of a terrorist attack. Consequently, special forces gather in a determined way to seek revenge for their deceased friends, calling their group "The Nameless," showing that they are not special and anyone in the country could make the same sacrifice for the continuity of the nation. The periphery continues to be the battleground for the awakening of the national self with militarized empowerment performed by the national coalition of forces.

3.4　*The Warrior*: The Resurgence of Republican Subjectivity

The first episode of *The Warrior* was broadcast on FOX TV on April 9, 2017. Owned by News Corporation based in the USA, FOX TV began its operations in Turkey in 2007. The corporation's broadcasting facilities focused on the production of soap operas and news bulletins, and soon became popular with news anchors including Fatih Portakal and İsmail Küçükkaya, whose critical reflections with a secularist emphasis against the government gained public recognition. Similar to *The Promise* and *The*

Nameless, The Warrior also attracted audience attention, faring well in the ratings and, as of December 2017, enjoying its second season while also maintaining 160,000 followers on its YouTube channel,[12] with its first episode receiving 2.5 million views online.[13]

Signaling a New Era with Reconciliation at the Center

The Warrior's main theme highlights significant differences as well as similarities with other productions. Similar to *The Promise* and *The Nameless*, *The Warrior* is also based on the formation of a group of special forces that decide to fight with the enemy figure after an initial crisis that hits and traumatizes the national self located at the center. Yet, different from the previously analyzed series where crises were set off by a terror attack, *The Warrior* puts forward a distinct initial crisis as its main narrative axis, the failed coup d'état attempt of July 15, 2016. In this regard, the series attempts to reconcile Kemalism with government policies (Atay 2017d) by centering its narrative on the role of Kemalist soldiers in thwarting the threats against the nation after July 15.

The first episode of *The Warrior* begins with a prison scene where former captain Kağan Bozok wakes from a nightmare recalling one of his past clashes in the mountains. His prison mate is Colonel Halil İbrahim Kopuz, a former soldier who was expelled from the army and sent to prison along with Kağan. Soon the narrative makes it known that the date is July 15, 2016, the night when a group of soldiers in the army attempt a coup d'état. The night of the coup attempt turns out to be risky for both soldiers since they are targeted by the coup plotters: as Halil is about to be stabbed by one of the prisoners, Kağan saves his life. With dramatic events unfolding, Halil observes that the coup plotters are specifically targeting him due to his love of the nation. He openly takes an anti-coup position by describing the soldiers attempting the coup as "inglorious people who imprisoned them with lies and now attacking the state." Watching the news on television showing real pictures of how civilians went out in the streets to stop the tanks, he says that as a soldier he is ashamed of those people calling themselves soldiers and massacring civilians.

---

[12] Savaşçı official YouTube channel is available at https://www.youtube.com/channel/UC7G8qP446Mwd3DwUQf_-N5w

[13] The first episode of Savaşçı is available at https://www.youtube.com/watch?v=DtWeoQ_-YP4

The Warrior's setting up of initial crises as the series' opening sequence illustrates a certain way of reading recent events. On the night of July 15, 2016 Turkey suffered a coup attempt that took the lives of 249 civilians. The series shows that the coup plotters do not limit themselves to this single event and that they have a history. Halil and Kağan are former members of the Turkish Army who were expelled and imprisoned by a group of army members and prosecutors linked to the coup plotters during the late 2000s. In this regard, the narrative makes an implicit reference to the *Ergenekon* and *Sledgehammer* trials held between 2007 and 2012. During this period, various members of the Turkish armed forces, predominantly Kemalists, were expelled from the army and accused of plotting a coup d'état against the government. The narrative does not openly state that there is any specific group responsible for these processes. However, it clearly implies that it is not the JDP government that undertook such injustices. Rather, Fetullah Gülen's group in the state is recognized as the perpetrator of the trials as well as for the July 15 coup attempt, which affirms the government discourse. As the series shows, these imprisoned Kemalist soldiers become allies of the government, uniting against the threats posed by the enemies of the nation.

Until this point in the narrative, the events are centered on the reformulation of the national self at the center following Turkey's recent political developments. Yet strikingly, it switches its attention to the periphery to fulfill this national self. Once the coup attempt is thwarted on the morning of July 16, Halil and Kağan's fate changes unexpectedly as they are summoned by the prison manager. The manager informs Halil of the events, describing the damage done to the army by coup plotters and that the army needs his services particularly for its military operations in the eastern part of Turkey. Since the army faces a serious crisis and it is still difficult to distinguish coup plotters from others, the chief of staff contends that the terrorists plan to use this disturbance to their advantage by attacking the peripheral cities. In response, Halil agrees to return to action on the condition that Kağan goes with him, as well as other members of a special team that he would put together. As the manager agrees to his demands, he tells Halil that, "Nobody will apologize for what you went though, you know that right?" Halil responds that, "Atatürk was sentenced to death during his independence struggle but he did not give up on his ideals for the nation." This conversation intensifies the particular narrative that points out the victimization of Kemalist soldiers, by highlighting that these soldiers are followers of Mustafa Kemal Atatürk and that they are and have always been motivated by their love of the nation. With the manager stating that, "It is not the day for our internal struggles," Halil agrees saying, "Who imprisoned us is not the state, but a group of people that attempts to destroy our state and cause a civil war." This scene signifies the moment when another coalition of national forces is formed similar to that in *The Nameless*. However, in *The Warrior* the emphasis is on the resurgence of Republican/Kemalist subjectivity. Halil soon gathers his team, consisting of former soldiers who were expelled from the army due to false accusations, most of whom are facing financial difficulties and experiencing psychological problems.

The Non-representation of the Peripheral Other

From this point an onwards, the narrative initiates a certain imagining of the periphery by focusing on Halil and Kağan's past experiences. Halil's wife was murdered by terrorists in the 1990s while he was serving in the region. Also, Kağan's father, who worked as a digger operator in a peripheral province, was murdered in a terrorist raid on a construction yard when he was a small child. In a dramatic flashback scene, Kağan saw terrorists murdering his father who hid him when the armed group arrived at the yard. These two past experiences are posited in the narrative as essential signifiers that constitute absolute victimization and legitimate ways of seeking revenge on the perpetrator. The periphery is positioned as the space that the terrorists—implicitly referring to the PKK—exploit with their attacks on civilians to weaken the Turkish state. In addition to the representation of such atrocities, there is no mention of the Kurdish problem, which would include various cultural or social experiences of ethnic identity and linguistic rights that Kurdish people might face in the region. Halil and Kağan are not interested in locating or solving such problems. Their core aim is to eliminate the threats posed against the state, which is experiencing serious trauma.

A significant motive enters the narrative just before Kağan is about to leave Ankara for his team's assignment—he meets Aslı, a female academic who holds anti-militarist views. Kağan watched Aslı commenting on television after the coup attempt, giving reasons why the military should stay away from politics and saying that the country needs to limit the authority of the military ideology in social, cultural and political spheres. She also supports liberties and freedoms with an anti-militarist and an anti-authoritarian stance. Kağan is frustrated and angered by her comments and the following day, while driving, he accidentally hits the back of Aslı's car causing some minor damage. The two characters meet and over subsequent episodes, Aslı falls in love with Kağan. This kind of transformation marks the moment when a gendered mechanism with regard to center–periphery dynamics is employed by the narrative. As opposed to the coherent, powerful, determined and militarized self attributed to Kağan, Aslı represents the corrupted self within the center, who lacks sufficient national will and enthusiasm to appreciate the center's military identity. As Kağan continues with his operations in the periphery, Aslı begins her transformation and correction. The struggle against the enemy in the periphery changes the antimilitarist person sitting in an ivory tower into the lover of a soldier.

Indeed, at the beginning of the narrative, Aslı is the only character who owns the necessary intellectual and critical means to examine the Kurdish issue, pointing out the problems of social and cultural exclusion that the Kurdish community encounters. However, this element is treated as a threat that could harm the series' hegemonic discourse on the peripheral other and is systematically eliminated by Aslı's falling in love with Kağan. The periphery cannot speak for itself in any of the military television series, yet certain representations manage to speak for the periphery in *The Promise* and *The Nameless*. However, the first episode of *The Warrior* indicates that the periphery cannot speak for itself and moreover, it is not allowed to be spoken for by representatives of the center's self. The periphery is unrepresented, but it is consumed by the center to fulfill a national identity. On the other hand, in a similar way to Bahar in *The Promise* who goes after Yavuz in Mardin so that she can be fulfilled, the narrative points at women's interpellation as a national militarized subject by the center's ideology, based on the military expeditions held in the periphery. This significant motive once again illustrates that the periphery constitutes the essential battleground not only for men to reinvest themselves as powerful subjects, but also for women to fulfill their national belonging by distancing themselves from demilitarized and apolitical circles that prevent the center realizing its true potential as a national subject.

As Kağan leads the eight man-strong special forces team on Halil's orders, the series narrates the experiences of the special forces team in seizing control of peripheral villages by thwarting any attacks. In one of the clashes, Kağan encounters the terrorist who murdered his father. This person becomes the object of revenge in following episodes. In addition, the team loses one member during a clash, and a martyrdom ceremony is held in his honor. The episode ends by highlighting the making of the militarist national self with the "commando oath" spoken by the special forces:

"I am a Turkish commando, I raze the enemy with my steel elbow, I am everywhere on air, land, sea, desert, always ready." In *The Warrior*, the periphery is considered solely in terms of a battleground without much emphasis on local people's reflections and perceptions of their identities. The militarization of the periphery becomes the strategy for the Republican/Kemalist subjectivity to reassert its presence at the center.

3.5 Conclusion

Produced and broadcast in late March and early April 2017, *The Promise*, *The Nameless* and *The Warrior* all reflect on Turkey's recent political developments. It is significant that these series are the first of their kind in the country's television history and they constitute crucial media representations to locate the boundaries of the self and the other, the center and the periphery in terms of militarized and nationalized subjectivities. All of these series narrate the atrocities perpetrated by various enemy figures and the subsequent formation of a special team of armed forces to counter the threats posed by these agents. As the locus of the terrorist acts, the periphery is a setting that needs to be taken under control to fulfill, regain the strength of, and reproduce the national self located at the center. In *The Promise*, the perpetrator is situated as the terrorist damaging the peaceful co-existence of the center and the periphery, identified as the West and the East respectively in a self-Orientalized manner. *The Nameless* extends the figure of the enemy to their internal and Western allies by illustrating the formation of a national coalition against them. *The Warrior* specifically deals with the resurgence of Republican/Kemalist soldiers and their increasing authority at the center recognized by their services at the periphery. Despite slight deviations in terms of the definitions of the self and the other, these series confirm the recent government discourse claiming that "there is no Kurdish issue, but a terrorism issue," since there is no mention of the possible cultural or social mechanisms of discrimination that the people of the region could be experiencing in terms of their rights. Contrarily, the peripheral subject is represented as loyal and obedient to the state, usually content with his/her life and the state's investments in the region, co-existing with the center in a peaceful way, occasionally with an exotic presence in Orientalist terms. It is the figure of the terrorist who threatens to destroy this co-existence, hence the special forces teams are formed to thwart this threat. Therefore, the periphery is the cultural other who is in need of being saved from the terrorist by the superior, secular, masculine and powerful self represented by the society's center.

Several critics argue that these series were produced due to pressure imposed on media corporations by the government (Aral 2017; Dizici 2017; Kılınçarslan 2017; Şalo 2017). In my analysis of these series, I agree that the representations closely reproduce the ideologies of nationalism and militarism, but I consider that evaluating these series as the mouthpieces of government would provide a limited understanding of the country's political and social landscape after 2015, particularly with regard to center–periphery relations. The kinds of cultural narratives that these television channels predominantly convey, especially via soap operas, reproduce a mainstream understanding of the lifestyles of secular Turks, rather than any Islamic signifiers that would refer to the social class represented by the government. In this regard, I consider these series as vehicles that the secularist, Republican or Kemalist center uses to re-establish itself in a privileged discursive position during the government's war on terror. The periphery at this point functions as a crucial discursive realm by which the center can regain its strength to solve the country's existing problems, mainly regarding the separatism associated with Kurdish armed groups. This makes the Kemalist social class an ally of the government rather than its enemy. The discourse aims to convince us that the government is in need of an inclusive national coalition, a repositioning of society's center with the co-operation of secular and conservative Turks, as opposed to their being common enemies. These series tend to generate the consent of conservative social classes regarding the merits of Kemalism, therefore they should not be considered as governmental interference in televisual discourse. On the contrary, they represent a move in televisual discourse dominated by secular Turks toward a repositioning within the center through dealing with the Kurdish periphery as the common cultural other.

Bibliography

Aral, E. (2017, March 20). Apoletli dizi seferberliği [A Wave of Military Series]. Retrieved from https://www.evrensel.net/yazi/78701/apoletli-dizi-seferberligi

Atay, T. (2017a, March 29). 'İsimsizler' ya da evet, evet, evet, evet! ['The Nameless' or Yes, Yes, Yes!]. Retrieved from http://www.cumhuriyet.com.tr/koseyazisi/708754/_isimsizler__ya_da_evet__evet__evet__evet_.html

Atay, T. (2017b, April 5). Referandum dizileri [Referendum Series]. Retrieved from http://www.cumhuriyet.com.tr/koseyazisi/713808/Referandum_dizileri.html

Atay, T. (2017c, April 7). 'SÖZ': PKK sana söylüyorum, IŞİD sen anla! ['THE PROMISE': PKK I Am Telling You, ISIS You Understand!]. Retrieved from http://www.cumhuriyet.com.tr/koseyazisi/715501/_SOZ___PKK_sana_soyluyorum__ISiD_sen_anla_.html

Atay, T. (2017d, April 12). 'Yeni Türkiye'ye Kemalist aşı denemesi: 'Savaşçı' [A Kemalist Vaccine Trial on 'New Turkey': 'The Warrior']. Retrieved from http://www.cumhuriyet.com.tr/koseyazisi/718767/_Yeni_Turkiye_ye_Kemalist_asi_denemesi___Savasci_.html?utm_source=partners&utm_medium=gazeteoku.com&utm_campaign=feed

Dizici, T. M. (2017, May 15). İsimsizler: Gençlerden elinizi çekin! [The Nameless: Take Your Hands Off the Youth!]. Retrieved from https://www.birgun.net/haber-detay/isimsizler-genclerden-elinizi-cekin-159566.html

Gunter, M. (2008). *The Kurds Ascending: The Evolving Solution to the Kurdish Problem in Iraq and Turkey*. New York: Palgrave Macmillan.

Heper, M. (2007). *The State and Kurds in Turkey: The Question of Assimilation*. Basingstoke/New York: Palgrave Macmillan.

Kardaş, T., & Balci, A. (2016). Inter-Societal Security Trilemma in Turkey: Understanding the Failure of the 2009 Kurdish Opening. *Turkish Studies*, *17*(1), 155–180.

Kılınçarslan, C. (2017, March 28). Üç "Terörle Mücadele" Dizisi Gösterimde: Neden Reyting mi? Siyaset mi? [Three "War on Terror" Series Broadcasting: Is Is Rating? Politics?]. Retrieved from https://m.bianet.org/bianet/siyaset/184930-uc-terorle-mucadele-dizisi-gosterimde-neden-reyting-mi-siyaset-mi

Şalo, F. (2017, April 6). Vatan Millet Kumanda [Nation, People and the Remote Control]. Retrieved from http://www.diken.com.tr/vatan-millet-kumanda/

CHAPTER 4

New Cultural Others? Unveiling the Limitations and Paradoxes

Abstract This chapter analyzes the manifestations of the cultural other in Turkish Airlines advertisements broadcast in Turkey in 2014 and 2015, and the cartoons of a popular humor magazine, *Misvak* published online in 2017. These works are important since they illustrate the ways in which social classes affiliated to the JDP government tend to represent themselves through the periphery as the cultural other. It is important to note that advertising and cartoon discourses have long been dominated by secularist imaginations, abstracted from religious or conservative lifestyles. Recent representations are important to show and problematize the ways in which the social classes, who have been excluded from the realm of popular culture, are now representing themselves at the center through the periphery in various ways—a process that unveils limitations and paradoxes. I argue that these representations highlight a crisis of cultural representation experienced by these social classes, which is evident in the ways in which the center–periphery dichotomy is shown in advertisements and the definition of the self through the depiction of cultural others is shown in cartoons.

Keywords Cartoon • Caricature • Advertising • Misogyny
• Speciesism • Racism

© The Author(s) 2018
A. Nas, *Media Representations of the Cultural Other in Turkey*,
https://doi.org/10.1007/978-3-319-78346-8_4

4.1 THE CONNECTEDNESS WITH THE PERIPHERAL OTHER

The emphasis on industrial and technological development has been a prominent discourse in Turkey's political history. Since the foundation of the nation-state in 1923, governments have been eager to promise economic advancement to their citizens with increased job opportunities, welfare and urban infrastructure. In particular, governments have made major attempts to improve the country's transport infrastructure, including roads, bridges and railways. The early Republican period witnessed the implementation of several programs to organize the national economy and develop the railways to maintain the interconnectedness of the country's provinces. Such an endeavor can be appreciated in the music of the "10th Year March" composed for the 10th anniversary of the nation-state's foundation, which is famous for the lines, "Demir ağlarla ördük anayurdu dört baştan" ["We knitted the motherland all across with iron networks"]. In this regard, the periphery was of utmost importance to the Republican elite as it had been constituted as a discourse that was both included in and excluded from the ideology of the nation-state.

Investment in transport technologies has also been a prominent policy of JDP governments. The party's main promise in terms of transport has been to improve the country's airline traffic system with the construction of airports in peripheral towns. With this aim, 29 airports were constructed in 15 years, increasing the number of passengers from 35 million to 180 million annually.[1] Turkish Airlines (THY), a government-sponsored company and Turkey's national flagship airline, is of great significance, as its transformation into a global brand during the JDP era has been the signifier of Turkey's economic growth and potential. Founded in 1933 as the State Airlines Administration, THY was modernized and turned into a brand in the 2000s, maintaining a fleet of 336 cargo and passenger airplanes, and is aiming to increase its operations to more than 500 airplanes by 2023.[2] The airline became a member of Star Alliance in 2008 and won Skytrax's Best Airline in Europe Award six consecutive times between 2011 and 2016. THY is also renowned for flying to many

---

[1] "Aslan: Türkiye'de havalimanı sayısı 55'e yükseldi" ["Aslan: The number of airports in Turkey has risen to 55"]. August 4, 2017. Anadolu Ajansı. Available: http://www.ensonhaber.com/aslan-turkiyede-havalimani-sayisi-55e-yukseldi.html, accessed December 15, 2017.

[2] "Turkish Airlines: About Us." Available: https://p.turkishairlines.com/tr-tr/basinodasi/hakkimizda/#tcm92-36323, accessed December 15, 2017.

global destinations (120 countries). Between 2004 and 2016, the airline's passenger numbers increased from 11.9 million to 62.7 million.[3] The company spent large amounts of money on advertising on a global scale, which led to the establishment of a THY brand. It sponsored major events including EURO 2016 (the European Football Championship) and Euroleague (the European Basketball League) as well as sponsoring the movie *Batman vs. Superman: Dawn of Justice* in 2016. Its earlier advertising campaigns starred global celebrities such as Lionel Messi, Kobe Bryant and Morgan Freeman.

Different from its global language addressing worldwide audiences, THY's advertising campaigns for national audiences address cultural notions, entailing various depictions of the cultural other through the narration of center and periphery. In particular, two advertising campaigns broadcast to national audiences regarding the construction of airports in Turkey's peripheral provinces—"Hayal Edince" ["Dream"], declaring the opening of Iğdır Airport in 2014 and "Vazgeçme" ["Do Not Give Up"], declaring the opening of Ordu-Giresun Airport in 2015,—propose significant narratives highlighting the kind of image that the brand projects towards the periphery.[4]

4.2 Imagining the Cultural Other in Turkish Airlines Advertisements

The Militarized Periphery in "Dream"

THY's first advertisement, entitled "Dream," was broadcast on television on April 23, 2014, and uploaded to the brand's official YouTube account on April 24, 2014.[5] The title of advertisement "Hayal Edince" is translated simply as "Dream." However, the word *Hayal* means "imagination," rather than dream, and so the title can be translated more properly as

---

[3] "Turkish Airlines: About Us." Available: https://p.turkishairlines.com/tr-tr/basin-odasi/hakkimizda/#tcm92-36323, accessed December 15, 2017.

[4] "Dream." April 24, 2014. Available: https://www.youtube.com/watch?v=oSD0YigRW3o, accessed February 6, 2018; "Do Not Give Up." Available: https://www.youtube.com/watch?v=vl3swM1hCeY, accessed February 6, 2018.

[5] "Dream." April 24, 2014. Available: https://www.youtube.com/watch?v=oSD0YigRW3o, accessed February 6, 2018.

"when one imagines," pointing at the kinds of imaginings actualized by the peripheral individuals of Iğdır province, a city of 80,000 people, located in Turkey's eastern Anatolian border. While the construction of Iğdır Airport was completed in July 2012, the advertisement was broadcast approximately two years after the opening of the airport, on April 23, 2014, which is celebrated in Turkey as "National Sovereignty and Children's Day," proclaimed by the early Republican regime with reference to the constitution of the national assembly in 1920, the founding parliament which would later declare the Republic of Turkey in 1923.

The advertisement portrays four local children speaking to each other in Turkish about the airplane that they can see flying over. Shown with English subtitles, the film initially announces that it is "dedicated to all children with big dreams," as it shows one of the children pointing at the airplane. The children, three male and one female, are dressed in traditional clothes and speak with local accents. The boy who points at the airplane asks, "Do you think that it is going to Istanbul?" The girl replies, "Where else would it go?" Another boy responds, "It is certain that it will not come here." The boy pointing at the airplane says enthusiastically, "I think it will come if we really want it to," as the children find themselves dreaming about the possibility that the airplane may land in their village. The introductory part of the advertisement offers a narrative that establishes an initial dichotomy between the center and the periphery through the representation of the cultural other. Semiotically, the children's appearances and their accents signify their *peripheralness* as opposed to the *centrality* of the brand. However, despite the Kurdish population in Iğdır, the children are not represented as Kurdish, but as rural Turks speaking in a distorted dialect. The way that the boy follows the route of the airplane with his finger is as if he dreams of catching it, illustrating the peripheral subject's desire to catch hold of recent improvements in technology. Concomitantly, his is an endeavor to meet with the center, to get acquainted with it by internalizing an unequal power relationship in which he participates. In this sense, the advertisement clearly establishes a power hierarchy between the center and the periphery as it portrays the center as something that is unreachable and unachievable, flying over the children and disregarding their desire to catch it. Moreover, the visual and semantic strategy that the advertisement puts forward in terms of representing the periphery as "children," highlights the reproduction of an Orientalist discourse, where the periphery is situated as the immature, childish, backward cultural other, as opposed to the technologically advanced and modern center represented by THY.

After the initial 15 seconds where the advertising discourse introduces the audience to the periphery as the cultural other, the narrative concentrates its focus on overcoming the particular problem that the peripheral subject experiences and hopes to solve—the possibility of making the airplane land in their village. The following scenes show the children making preparations to construct a playground airport. They pick up stones to mark the boundaries and draw lines in the soil and write "Iğdır Airport." They construct an air traffic control tower using desks and wooden ladders, on which they hang a small Turkish flag. They then wait for the airplanes. When they see one flying over, they react with excitement, "Oh my God, it is coming, look over here, we are down here!" They are disappointed when they see the airplane disappear into the distance. While the children's initial attempt to actualize the landing of the airplane ends in failure, the narrative strengthens the center–periphery dichotomy with its visual manifestation of the children's efforts. The children are joyful in their building of a play airport. Their endeavor potentially gives the audience (the urban middle classes) pleasure, as they identify themselves with the center. However, what the children are going through can be read as a schizophrenic experience. They engage with the airplane and break ties with reality, longing for the actualization of an impossibility. In this regard, their reaction to the airplane flying over heightens the center–periphery distinction. The way the children act—yelling at the airplane—might appear as if they are seeking help to *survive* their peripheral conditions.

As the children's attempts to be seen by the airplane continue, they have a brilliant idea that is sparked by a local wedding: they use electric lights to illuminate their airfield. The introduction of a cultural narrative through a brief local wedding ceremony scene with traditional music, extends to the overall signifying practices with regard to the Orientalist formula that underscores the traditional lifestyle of the periphery, devoid of any ethnic markers. Later, the children turn on the airfield lights at night when the airplane passes by and yell to the skies, "We are over here!" Their failure to attract the attention of the airplane results in even more disappointment, as one of the boys desperately complains, "It is not coming." Shortly after the Sun rises, the children see the THY airplane descend and approach them. We see one of the boys saluting the approaching airplane like a soldier, standing on the air traffic control tower waving a Turkish flag, while the children excitedly celebrate the arrival of the airplane. This signifier involves a military symbol: the child welcomes the airplane with a salute, identifying himself as a soldier. The power hierarchy between the center and the periphery is further emphasized with this particular image of the child. As a representative of the periphery, the child is militarized, treated as an obedient soldier, approving and celebrating the authority of the center. The semiotic distribution of signifiers in terms of their visual arrangement shows the child saluting into the camera—that is, to the airplane—which helps the audience identify itself with THY, contrary to the cultural other.

THY's "Dream" advertisement ends with the airplane landing at Iğdır Airport and being welcomed on the runway by locals carrying Turkish flags and "Welcome to Iğdır" banners. As one of the boys says, "Finally it came," while looking toward the aircrew who are approaching, a handsome uniformed pilot recognizes the boy and salutes him while he walks along the runway. As his salute is met with the smiles of the children, the narrative clinches the final stage of the children's interpellation by the nationalist and militarist ideology represented by the center. The narrator remarks, "What is the point of flying to most destinations around the world, if we don't fly everywhere in Turkey?" The THY advertisement is a clear manifestation of the way in which the periphery is imagined by the center; an image that entails the ideological interpellation of the peripheral subject through militarist and nationalist impulses.

After its release, the advertisement met with a positive public response. The children starring in the advertisement appeared on television shows, including the popular *Beyaz Show*, and were interviewed by several newspapers. In the media, the advertisement was soon referred to as "the advertisement that pulled Turkey's heartstrings,"[6] as the commentaries focused on the children, who were villagers themselves, getting on the airplane for the first time during the shooting of the advertisement.[7] Although the children were from Antalya province and not Iğdır, this was not a problem for mainstream media and the public. In this respect, the advertisement was pure *simulacrum*, which posed a certain imagination of

---

[6] "Türkiye'nin konuştuğu reklamda ilginç ayrıntı!" ["Interesting detail in the advertisement that Turkey speaks about"]. April 25, 2014. Gazete Vatan. Available: http://www.gazetevatan.com/turkiye-nin-konustugu-reklamda-ilginc-ayrinti--631156-gundem/, accessed December 15, 2017.

[7] "THY Iğdır Havaalanı reklam çocukları konuştu" ["Children in THY's Iğdır Airport advertisement spoke"]. April 28, 2014. CNN Turk. Available: https://www.cnnturk.com/haber/turkiye/thy-igdir-havaalani-reklami, accessed December 15, 2017.

the periphery as the reality in Jean Baudrillard's terms (1994). Considered together with the company's later advertisement, "Do Not Give Up," "Dream" points out the paradoxes and inadequacies that the JDP era manifests in terms of cultural representation. As a government that claims to be the representative of the periphery over the center, the advertising language of a government-sponsored company tends to constitute the periphery as the cultural other.

The Elimination of Peripheral Resistance in "Do Not Give Up"

THY's "Do Not Give Up" advertisement was broadcast on television and online in June 2015,[8] after the official opening of Ordu-Giresun Airport on May 22, 2015, which was attended by President Erdoğan.[9] The airport project was treated with special care by the government since it was declared to be Europe's first and the world's third airport located on an artificial island constructed on the sea. Ordu-Giresun Airport was significant for the government as it portrayed the technological advancement of the country in terms of increased transport networks between the center and the periphery.

The advertisement begins by showing a football pitch in a village, where male children are training. A man approaches the field and calls out to the children, "I have good news, we are going to the finals by airplane!" The camera then shows the goalkeeper, İlyas, who is surprised by the news and responds in anger, "By airplane? How come?" Confronted by İlyas's temper, his fellow teammate asks, "Are you afraid?" He responds, "Why would I be afraid? I am not coming." The following scene shows İlyas spending time at home with his family, watching the news on television about the opening of Ordu-Giresun Airport with the first flight of THY. İlyas watches the news with disinterest. The following scenes show İlyas's friends helping him to get over his phobia of flying.

In the advertisement, we see a similar strategy that was employed in "Dream." The peripheral subjects are villagers with traditional clothing and local accents. As children, they signify a lack of power and of fulfillment.

---

[8] "Do Not Give Up." Available: https://www.youtube.com/watch?v=vl3swM1hCeY, accessed February 6, 2018.

[9] "Ordu-Giresun Havalimanı Açıldı" ["Ordu-Giresun Airport Opened"]. May 22, 2015. NTV. Available: https://www.ntv.com.tr/ekonomi/ordu-giresun-havalimani-acildi,4Rs9FuUthEmxziBIecWLhw, accessed December 15, 2017.

Different from the previous advertisement, the narrative concentrates on the struggle of one character, İlyas, who is fearful of flying. The initial dichotomy between the center and the periphery is already set by associating a certain backwardness to the periphery as opposed to the modernizing force of the center. Whereas peripheral agents other than İlyas are ready to enjoy their modernization, İlyas resists the kind of empowering narrative imposed on him by the center's privileged and superior gaze. The narrative shows this as a problem to be solved rather than a form of resistance against subjection.

In the following scenes we see İlyas's friends making various efforts to help İlyas to overcome his phobia. İlyas makes timid efforts to climb ladders and cross bridges. He continuously checks on his situation, "I will not fall down, will I? Is this safe?" After a series of efforts, İlyas manages to meet the challenges he is faced with. After his success, the narrative switches its focus to the airport where the team gathers to board the airplane, but without İlyas. When the last call for boarding is made and the aircrew prepare to depart, İlyas appears and runs toward the airplane from the departure hall. İlyas makes it onto the flight at the very last minute and his teammates and passengers celebrate. In this final scene, the narrator says "For Turkey, who sees no obstacles to achieving its goals, to connect with every corner of the country easily," as the camera shows the airplane departing from Ordu-Giresun Airport. The advertisement ends with three elderly female villagers looking in the direction of the departing airplane and whistling, with the subtitles displaying, "Do not give up son."

Similar to "Dream", "Do Not Give Up" also imagines the peripheral individual in accordance with the superior gaze of the center. Iğdır province is an area with a relatively small population but Ordu and Giresun are large urban areas—Ordu has a population of 700,000 and Giresun has 400,000 residents. Despite their large urban populations, the advertisement imagines these geographies as rural areas, characterized by traditional clothes and housing as signifiers of a village lifestyle. By Orientalizing the region, THY again asserts its presence over the peripheral subject as a modern, technologically advanced brand, situating itself as the representative of the nation's core ambitions for development. Within this narrative of development, İlyas appears as a defiant character, whose resistance is neutralized and eliminated by the enlightening ideology of the center. In both advertisements, the villagers serve as voluntary participants of the subjection that they are exposed to. İlyas's friends make crucial efforts to help him overcome his fear, or in other words, so that İlyas can end his resistance and agree to be a voluntary participant in the center's enlightening gaze. This motive in the narrative beautifully illustrates Michel Foucault's famous description of the surveillance mechanism of the panoptic model, where prisoners "become the principles of their own subjection" (Foucault 1995, p. 203), reckoning the productive operations of power relations by which the peripheral individual subjectifies himself/herself. What follows is İlyas's celebration as he boards the airplane. He becomes a proper individual and a citizen by leaving aside his resistance. Finally, the expressions of the villager women, encouraging İlyas not to give up, further establish the peripheral subject's voluntary subjection via technologies of power exercised by the superior center. This particular scene bears a crucial symbol, as the women whistle at the airplane, rather than speaking—a perfect illustration of Spivak's famous question, "Can the subaltern speak?" In the advertisement, the subaltern is deprived of the means of speaking for himself/herself; he/she merely exists as a cultural other subjected to the imaginations of the superior, modernizing and enlightening gaze of the center.

Interestingly, the subalterns in Iğdır and in Ordu and Giresun embody the JDP's main voters. The government-affiliated THY advertisements highlight a certain crisis in terms of cultural representation that JDP experiences—a problem resonating in the words of Erdoğan, who stated in May 2017 that "[we] managed to gain political power but failed to establish cultural power." The advertisements echo the tendencies of the early Republican elite to approach the periphery as a backward, non-modern, traditional cultural other who is in need of advancement, and actualized by the Republican elite by means of the increased ways of connectedness. Therefore, according to the THY advertisement, the JDP-affiliated social classes mimic the Republican ideology and its positional superiority over the periphery by identifying themselves with the central/privileged position of the old regime. Yet, this is the very position that subjectifies these social classes, whose peripheral reactions paved the way for the formation of the JDP. The advertisements can also be regarded as a continuation of the mainstream advertising discourse in Turkey that systematically acts as the voice of the center by concealing, objectifying or Orientalizing the peripheral other, as described in the introductory chapter with regard to the dominant inclinations in the advertising discourse (Sect. 1.5.5). I argue that this kind of representation highlights a crisis that the JDP faces in terms of representing itself through popular culture in an original way, other than the already existing definitions and discourses on the self and the other, the center and the periphery. The deprivation of a certain set of definitions and discourses that would replace the existing ones is closely related to the inadequacies that the JDP-affiliated social classes face in terms of representing themselves in popular culture with sophistication. The next section will explore such limitations as illustrated by *Misvak* magazine.

4.3 Between Misogyny and Speciesism: The Cultural Others in *Misvak* Cartoons

Cartoon as a Field of Power Relations

Since the turn of the century, the satirical language of humor magazines met with harsh responses from government officers. Erdoğan has sued magazines, claiming that the cartoons were an assault on his personality, among other reasons (Aviv 2013). Historically, the kinds of representations engaged by cartoonists have reflected the perspectives of a central subject as opposed to the periphery, especially with the flow of migration to industrial centers such as Istanbul since the 1950s with cartoons depicting the peripheral individual in vulgar, non-modern and disproportionate ways, indicating the individual's failure to adapt to modern urban life with *Hacıağa* and *Mağanda* cartoons (Öncü 1999, 2002). Such a central outlook to this sphere of popular culture paved the way for a certain hegemony to be established in terms of the images and the discourses that these cartoonists circulate among their readers. In this regard, the narratives that these magazines engage in are characterized by an exclusion of any signifiers that would correspond to the promotion of conservative or Islamic lifestyles, characterizing the peripheral other. Therefore it is possible to observe that despite the JDP's rise to power in 2002 and its later election victories, the cultural identity that the JDP represented along with conservative and Islamic motives constituted the underrepresented cultural others in popular manifestations, especially in cartoons.

Although the JDP won the majority of the vote, it could not see itself as the majority in the sphere of cultural production in terms of cartoons. Conversely, after 2002 many cartoonists published satirical materials that criticized Erdoğan. The first tension between Erdoğan and the cartoonists occurred when, in May 9, 2004, Musa Kart from *Cumhuriyet* newspaper drew an Erdoğan caricature showing him as a cat, wrapped up in threads, saying "Do not create tension, we promised that we will solve the Imam-Hatip issue," which resulted in Erdoğan suing Kart for assaulting his dignity.[10] Subsequently, in 2005, *Penguen* magazine published a cover page depicting Erdoğan disguised as various animals and criticizing the fine that Musa Kart was ordered to pay in court (40,000 Turkish Liras).[11] Although the court dropped the case due to insufficient evidence, tension between the cartoonists and Erdoğan continued throughout the 2000s. In December 2013, Musa Kart was once again sued over a similar allegation when he drew a caricature of Erdoğan saying, "No worries, our guard is a hologram," referring to corruption claims (Tremblay 2014). In 2015, *Penguen* caricaturists Bahadır Baruter and Özer Aydoğan were sentenced to ten months in prison for their satirical cover published by the magazine after Erdoğan's election as president in August 2014, with Erdoğan portrayed as entering the presidential palace saying, "At least we should have cut a journalist," referring to the religious tradition of sacrificing an animal as thanks to God for an achievement (Usta 2015). Confronted by charges since the mid-2000s, cartoonists have continuously denied the allegations based on freedom of speech, further underscoring that a prime minister or a president of the country should be more tolerant of criticism.

In the last decade, satirical magazines such as *Bayan Yanı*, *Gırgır*, *Leman*, *Ot*, *Penguen* and *Uykusuz* have been widely circulated, holding critical stances against the government (van het Hof 2015, p. 32). Alongside minor Islamist cartoon magazines such as *Fit*, *Filit*, *Cümbür*, *Cıngar*, *Ustura* and *Dinazor* throughout the 1990s, *Cafcaf* has hit back (from 2007), countering the domination of secular, leftist caricature discourse (Çolak 2016, p. 237). In 2008, *Cafcaf* claimed that it was continuing its operations independently, preferring to portray the social and political problems of conservative social classes (Çolak 2016, p. 238). With the outbreak of Gezi activism in June 2013, satire has been employed as a major narrative strategy by activists in public spaces and online environments, which highlights the increasing importance of artistic manifestations, including cartoons, as discursive sites for hegemonic struggle (Şener 2013, p. 41; Yalcintas 2015, p. 7).

---

[10] "Yargıtay karikatür kararını bozdu" ["Supreme Court cancels the cartoon decision"]. April 18, 2006. Mynet. Available: http://www.mynet.com/haber/guncel/yargitay-karikatur-kararini-bozdu-232841-1, accessed December 25, 2017.

[11] "Kediden bugüne Erdoğan karikatürleri" ["Erdoğan caricatures since the cat until today"]. November 10, 2010. NTV. Available: https://www.ntv.com.tr/galeri/turkiye/kediden-bugune-Erdoğan-karikaturleri,eOPwUeUSoEiLswya6BBM_Q, accessed December 25, 2017.

In 2015, *Misvak* appeared as an alternative cartoon magazine with caricaturists from Islamist backgrounds. Publishing cartoons online on the magazine's Facebook account, *Misvak* managed to gain more than 480,000 followers in two years.[12] Different from previously published magazines affiliated with Islamist circles, *Misvak* proved itself to be the most popular of the cartoon magazines created, maintaining an explicit support of Erdoğan, while at the same time being accused of promoting hate speech by its critics. The magazine has been considered by the pro-government *Yeni Akit* newspaper, known for its hate speeches toward non-Muslims and secular groups (Gümüş and Dural 2012), as an effort that "successfully challenges *Penguen*."[13] Accordingly, *Misvak* was considered as an attempt to challenge secularist/leftist hegemony in the cartoon realm. In Pierre Bourdieu's (1984) term, cartoon constitutes a "field" consisting of the complex interplay of power relations that distinct social classes compete according to their cultural capitals and habituses.

Misvak's cartoons involve three different layers of meaning: the promotion of xenophobic content through the depiction of anti-Western sentiments; countering secularism by the degradation of certain icons and behaviors associated with secular social classes; and the advocacy of a discourse of Turkish nationalism essentially through the otherization of the figures related to Kurds. *Misvak* cartoonists actualize these meanings by implementing certain narrative strategies based on misogyny, racism, homophobia, militarism and speciesism. These strategies provide *Misvak* with the necessary discursive space for self-representation through the demonstration of the cultural other.

Anti-Western Sentiment

Misvak cartoons tend to reproduce a nationalist, Islamist self as opposed to internal and external enemies. In this regard, Turkey is conceived of as a country surrounded by plots conducted by Western countries, including the USA, the United Kingdom and Germany. Internal agents, such as the main opposition Republican People's Party (RPP) and the pro-Kurdish People's Democratic Party (PDP), are claimed to support these external agents. A cartoon published on October 6, 2017, illustrates the capture of PKK members in Turkey's Muğla province (Fig. 4.1). Four men are lying on the ground wearing female underwear, made from the national flags of

---

[12] Misvak's official Facebook page: https://www.facebook.com/misvakdergi
[13] "Misvak dergisi Penguen'e taş çıkartıyor" ["Misvak is surpassing Penguen"]. September 13, 2015. Yeni Akit. Available: http://www.yeniakit.com.tr/haber/misvak-mizah-dergisi-penguene-tas-cikartiyor-93410.html, accessed: December 25, 2017.

Fig. 4.1 A misogynistic cartoon by *Misvak*. (Retrieved from https://www.facebook.com/misvakdergi/photos/a.1668212910067998.1073741829.1668161890073100/2006184012937551/?type=3 on February 8, 2018)

the USA, Israel and Germany. Initiating a particular narrative suggesting that the West is the absolute enemy, the figure of the enemy is portrayed as female as opposed to the Turkish masculine superior self. Narrating the West as the cultural other, the cartoon makes a collection of enemy figures in the form of women, hence attempting a misogynist symbol as its main narrative strategy.

In another cartoon published on October 10, 2017, a soldier in traditional Ottoman military dress yells at enemy figures consisting of PKK, ISIS and YPG ("People's Protection Units", the Kurdish militia in Syria), swinging his sword saying, "We can come at night all of a sudden." The militants are portrayed as unwilling and too frightened to fight the Turkish soldier, yet they are pushed to do so by a crusader figure, representing the Western subject. They say to the crusader, "Why don't you fight like a man?" and the crusader replies, "Like a man? What does that mean?" The cartoon illustrates the co-operation of terrorist organizations with the West who together plot against Turkey. The misogynistic remarks attribute a masculine image to the Turkish soldier and associate the "cowardice" of the enemy figure with being female.

Finally, a cartoon published on November 12, 2017, portrays a young man picking up fruit in a grocery shop, dressed in a gown decorated with the flag of the USA. Wearing an ear-ring and representing a secular, Western figure, the young man takes fruit from a category "the West's unseen face" and places it next to "the West's seen face." The West's seen face is composed of civilization, science and freedom, whereas its unseen face includes prostitution, atheism, egoism and materialism. The young man represents a secular subject who has been deceived by the West and has fallen at the hands of a destructive civilization. Supported by misogynist and masculinist narratives, *Misvak* cartoons reproduce an Occidentalist discourse that precisely manifests the West as the absolute enemy.

The Secular Other and Speciesism

The second layer of meaning that characterizes *Misvak*'s discourse is related to the ways in which the magazine negotiates its distance from the secular other. In this regard, the main opposition party, the RPP, can be observed in several cartoons as the cultural other. The RPP and its leader, Kemal Kılıçdaroğlu, who undertook a *March for Justice* from Ankara to Istanbul from June 15 to July 9, 2017 to protest the government's misuses in the state of emergency, is the cartoon's central motive. Kılıçdaroğlu's oppositional stance serves as a major concern for *Misvak* caricaturists, who illustrate him as a political figure allying with the West to plot against Erdoğan. The RPP is targeted by *Misvak* caricaturists through implicit representations that aim to provoke anti-Mustafa Kemal Atatürk sentiments. In February 2017, the magazine published a cartoon illustrating three donkey-like figures looking at a statue of a donkey stating, "This is our holy donkey, we would all become donkeys if he did not exist."[14] The narrative is a reaction against making sculpture, which is considered a sin by Islam due to the inappropriateness of representing a person that God has created, as well as against the supporters of Kemalism, who frequently claim that Turks would not exist if Atatürk did not save them.

[14] "Misvak dergisinden tepki çeken karikatür" ["Misvak caricature draws reaction"]. February 18, 2017. T24. Available: http://t24.com.tr/haber/misvak-dergisinden-tepki-ceken-karikatur,389518, accessed: December 25, 2017.

Misvak's anti-Kemalism was once more manifest in a cartoon published on November 6, 2017, prior to the November 10 anniversary of Atatürk's death. A famous slogan of the Kemalists states "My ancestor, we follow your lead," referring to the ideals set by Mustafa Kemal Atatürk as appropriated from the Ottoman Sultan Abdülhamid II. The cartoon portrays Abdülhamid II, an autocrat with Islamist policies and the last sultan of the Ottoman Empire, overthrown by the Young Turk Revolution of 1908, as the true ancestor of the conservative social classes instead of Atatürk. Anti-secular tendencies were shown by several other cartoons that recommended that viewers transform their daily language and use Arabic words instead of Turkish words, such as "Selamınaleyküm" instead of Turkish "Günaydın" [good morning] and "Mübarek" instead of "Kutlu" [blessed]. Eventually, a historical narrative is combined with an anti-RPP position to isolate secular signifiers from the social sphere by the restoration of an Islamist vocabulary that is manifested through several icons. In this regard, homophobia is employed as a narrative strategy that *Misvak* employs to otherize RPP. On November 11, 2017, a cartoon reacted against the RPP mayor of Bursa's Nilüfer province who decided to pass a local regulation to reserve a 20% quota for sexual minorities in village councils. Depicting the mayor as talking to the LGBT+ community, "This country needs you," the cartoon mocks LGBT+ individuals, treating them as if they are not worthy subjects of the nation.

In addition to the anti-Western sentiments and anti-secular attempts, the emphasis on Turkish nationalism occupies an important motive in *Misvak* cartoons. In this regard, the PDP and its former leader, Selahattin Demirtaş, are frequently referred to as an internal enemy who co-operates with the West and threaten the nation's unity. On September 25, 2017, Erdoğan warned Mesud Barzani—the former leader of the Kurdish autonomous region in Iraq who decided to hold a referendum for independence—to withdraw the referendum or "they would come over there all of a sudden at night.", hinting at a military intervention to Iraq. On October 5, 2017, *Misvak* published a cartoon showing Erdoğan and Devlet Bahçeli—leader of the Nationalist Movement Party (NMP) and a supporter of Erdoğan's policies—driving a "white Toros," the kind of vehicle associated with the killers of many Kurdish activists and civilians throughout the 1990s (Brakel 2016, p. 1) (Fig. 4.2). With license plates of "82" and "83" signifying Mosul and Kirkuk provinces—longed for as Turkey's future cities by capturing them from Iraq—the cartoon manifests a military fantasy with an emphasis on the destruction of Kurdish identity

Fig. 4.2 "White Toros" cartoon. (Retrieved from "*Misvak* put Erdoğan on White Toros for Conquest" http://www.diken.com.tr/misvak-erdogani-beyaz-torosa-bindirip-fetihe-cikardi/on February 7, 2018)

in the region. Another cartoon published on November 3, 2017, shows an armed figure connoting the imprisoned PKK leader, Abdullah Öcalan, standing on one side of a traditional weighing scales, with the other side containing a dog. The mechanism is called "honor scale" as it shows that the dog weighs more than the enemy figure—a speciesist comment.

It is striking to observe that speciesism is a common strategy that *Misvak* cartoonists use to imply the cultural other in terms of anti-Western and anti-secular sentiments. Though it is a common strategy to use animal figures in cartoons as metaphors, *Misvak* cartoons actualize this merely for the purpose of giving offense. In a cartoon published on October 18,

NEW CULTURAL OTHERS? UNVEILING THE LIMITATIONS AND PARADOXES 87

Fig. 4.3 Speciesism in a *Misvak* cartoon. (Retrieved from https://www. facebook.com/misvakdergi/photos/a.1668170840072205.1073741828. 1668161890073100/2011868162369136/?type=3&theater on February 8, 2018)

2017, Can Dündar, former chief editor of oppositional daily newspaper *Cumhuriyet*, is portrayed as a dog that is owned by German chancellor Angela Merkel (Fig. 4.3). Referencing the show dogs that appear with their trainers in the television program *Turkey's Got Talent*, the cartoon shows Merkel telling the jury members, "I am attending the show from Germany. Together we will see how this German hybrid Coni (Can) obeys my rules without any question." Dündar was targeted by government officials due to the special news coverage that he published in May 2014 about the Turkish intelligence service's secret weapon transfer to Syria, allegedly to radical Islamist groups. The government fiercely rejected the claims and accused Dündar of espionage. Faced with a trial and a period of imprisonment, Dündar left Turkey and settled in Germany—an act that a *Misvak* cartoon described as a further act of betrayal, reducing Dündar to the status of an animal as the signifier of an obedient object owned by Western powers that plot against Turkey.

In addition to speciesist comments that intersect with an anti-Western narrative, *Misvak* also attempts to forge an anti-secularist response in its followers by tending to degrade RPP affiliated opponents by portraying them as animals. Another cartoon published on September 4, 2017, portrays a conversation between two men, one saying, "*Sözcü* newspaper wrote that the presidential palace should be converted into a stable in RPP rule," as the other responds, "They don't have to make a special effort, if they live there for two days, it will turn into a stable." The magazine also portrays the students of Middle East Technical University (METU)—an outspoken group of anti-government activist—as donkey figures in two different cartoons. The first cartoon stated that no matter how well they graduate, they still remain as "donkeys" and the second cartoon claims that METU is funded by the US government showing Donald Trump giving USD 850,000 to a donkey figure saying "We do not give money to a donkey that we will not kiss." The donkey responds "Surely my owner, my body your decision." *Misvak* cartoons frequently employ speciesism to mark the inferiority of the cultural other that refers to society's secularist, leftist social segments, accused of plotting against a government allied with foreign forces.

4.4 Conclusion

This chapter addresses the problems and the limitations of cultural representation in popular culture delivered by agents affiliated with the dominant political ideology in Turkey throughout the 2010s. The analysis of Ordu-Giresun and Iğdır Airport advertisements highlight the paradoxes by which THY, a government-affiliated brand, tends to establish a power hierarchy between the center that it represents—with regard to its technological advancements—and the periphery, as the non-modern other. Such a representation involves a paradox since the JDP claims to be a supporter of the periphery, while through its advertisements the company reproduces a power hierarchy against the peripheral subject. It could be argued that the advertisements mimic the definitions of the center–periphery dichotomy that existed prior to a JDP government, a Republican narrative that situates the periphery as the non-modern other, which highlights the crisis that the JDP-related social classes encounter in terms of cultural representation.

This chapter's second focus is on the representations of the cultural other in *Misvak* magazine. *Misvak* includes various narratives by which one can capture insights into Turkey's ruling ideology in the second half of 2010s and its contemporary implications. *Misvak* cartoons show that the social class of caricaturists who associate themselves with the ruling party tend to define themselves and their goals based on establishing enemy figures rather than offering coherent, sophisticated and original narratives that would illustrate their worldviews. Accordingly, the members of a social class who were once peripheralized, otherized and dismissed as undesirable citizens of Republican elitism, begin to establish a space at the center of power relations, concomitantly with inaugurating discursive mechanisms that peripheralize and otherize certain notions and social classes, including the West, secularists and Kurdish opposition. It is not possible to understand what their ideology offers as a worldview, since the cartoons are deprived of the necessary narrative strategies to construct substantial and sophisticated arguments on the kind of values that this social class maintains. Rather, the cartoons proceed through a superficial critique of Western civilization, secularism and Kurds, with overtly political statements basing their narratives on misogyny, homophobia, racism, militarism and speciesism. *Misvak* manages to mobilize its followers based on insistent representations of the cultural other, yet at the same time its existence rests on a paradox that it requires the cultural other to persist and define itself in popular culture.

Bibliography

Aviv, E. E. (2013). Cartoons in Turkey – From Abdülhamid to Erdoğan. *Middle Eastern Studies, 49*(2), 221–236.

Baudrillard, J. (1994). *Simulacra and Simulation*. Ann Arbor: University of Michigan Press.

Bourdieu, P. (1984). *Distinction: A Social Critique of the Judgement of Taste*. Cambridge, MA: Harvard University Press.

Brakel, K. (2016). The Resurfacing Turkish-Kurdish Question and Its Regional Impact. *DGAPkompakt*, (12), 1–6. Retrieved from https://dgap.org/en/think-tank/publications/dgapanalyse-compact/resurfacing-turkish-kurdish-question-and-its-regional

Çolak, E. (2016). İslam ile Görsel Mizah: Türkiye'de İslami Mizah Dergiciliğinin Dönüşümü [Islam and Visual Humor: Transformation of the Islamic Humor Magazine Publishing in Turkey]. *Moment Dergi, 3*(1), 228–247.

Foucault, M. (1995). *Discipline and Punish: The Birth of the Prison* (trans: Sheridan, A.). New York: Vintage Books.

Gümüş, B., & Dural, A. B. (2012). Othering Through Hate Speech: The Turkish-Islamist (V)AKIT Newspaper as a Case Study. *Turkish Studies, 13*(3), 489–507.

Öncü, A. (1999). Istanbulites and Others: The Cultural Cosmology of 'Middleness' in the Era of Neo-liberalism. In Ç. Keyder (Ed.), *Istanbul: Between the Global and the Local* (pp. 95–119). New York: St. Martins.

Öncü, A. (2002). Global Consumerism, Sexuality as Public Spectacle, and the Cultural Remapping of Istanbul in the 1990s. In A. S. Deniz Kandiyoti (Ed.), *Fragments of Culture: The Everyday of Modern Turkey* (pp. 171–190). London/New York: I.B. Tauris.

Şener, Ö. (2013). The Gezi Protests, Polyphony and 'Carnivalesque Chaos'. *Journal of Global Faultlines, 1*(2), 40–42.

Tremblay, P. (2014, November 4). Caricatures of Erdogan Flood Twitter. Retrieved from https://www.al-monitor.com/pulse/originals/2014/10/turkey-cartoonists-unite-against-erdogan.html

Usta, A. (2015, October 25). Turkish Cartoonists Sentenced to Jail for Insulting Erdoğan. Retrieved from http://www.hurriyetdailynews.com/turkish-cartoonists-sentenced-to-jail-for-insulting-erdogan-80145

van het Hof, S. D. (2015). Political Potential of Sarcasm: Cynicism in Civil Resentment. In A. Yalcintas (Ed.), *Creativity and Humour in Occupy Movements: Intellectual Disobedience in Turkey and Beyond* (pp. 30–47). London: Palgrave Macmillan.

Yalcintas, A. (2015). Intellectual Disobedience in Turkey. In A. Yalcintas (Ed.), *Creativity and Humour in Occupy Movements: Intellectual Disobedience in Turkey and Beyond* (pp. 6–29). London: Palgrave Macmillan.

CHAPTER 5

Toward a Conclusion: Imagining the Cultural Other

Abstract This book is an attempt to problematize the representations of the cultural other in Turkey through the analysis of media representations based on the country's long-running conflict between center and periphery. In doing so, I cover a variety of media representations including film narratives, television series, advertising and cartoons that were published during the 2010s and argue that the media constitutes a conflicting field of power relations between JDP-affiliated social classes and other segments of society. Turkey's political situation particularly since the turn of the century may give the impression that the JDP, which was once a representative of the periphery, now occupies the center by consolidating its power. By problematizing this particular perception, I highlight a crisis in cultural hegemony and argue that the media provides a crucial realm for distinct agents, ranging from feminist filmmakers to pro-JDP cartoonists, to define the cultural other by imagining it in different ways. To conclude, the Turkish experience shows that the center and the periphery should be considered as discourses characterized by a dynamic interplay of power relations, rather than as fixed positions occupied by certain social classes.

Keywords Center • Periphery • JDP (AKP) • Cultural capital • Homophobia • Hegemony

In this book, I attempt to provide an up-to-date analysis of media representations concerned with the imagining of the cultural other in Turkey through films, television series, advertisements and cartoons produced between 2013 and 2018. In doing so, I highlight the complex ways in which the sphere of culture functions for various social classes as a crucial realm where they can exercise technologies of power through defining the cultural other. In this respect, the imagining of the periphery becomes a strategic instrument for a variety of agents to discursively establish themselves in media representations. Turkey's long-running center–periphery conflict is reproduced and reformulated by various representations in visual culture by the social classes who invest their privileged gaze from the center and direct it toward the cultural other located at the periphery.

Although the JDP's consolidation of political power since 2002 as the representative of the periphery gives the impression that center–periphery hierarchies have eroded and the periphery now occupies the center, media representations highlight the complexity of discourses in which different social agents participate to define themselves through the imagining of distinct peripheries. These agents include feminist filmmakers, secular Turks producing military television series and pro-JDP cartoonists and advertisers, whose common effort is to imagine the cultural other in accordance with their hegemonic intentions formed by distinct emancipatory agendas. The narratives constituted by these social classes portray the distinct ways in which these groups locate themselves as the enlightened and the empowered self at the center, dealing with the problems of the other for various purposes including self-realization, self-fulfillment and progress. I argue that the center and the periphery show a diversity of identities and social classes rather than stable and fixed entities. Centers and peripheries are *imagined* geographies and identities. The sphere of culture in Turkey should be analyzed with a critical attitude that reveals the complex power relations exercised through media. Though it cannot be disputed that the JDP's dominance in the political sphere effects the sphere of culture in various ways, one should note that media representations in film, advertising, television and cartoons constitute a complex field where different social agents—including feminists, secular Turks, Kemalists, left-wing caricaturists and pro-JDP advertisers or cartoonists—all participate in a hegemonic struggle to retain positions at the center.

In this respect, the crucial question arises whether the periphery as the cultural other can or cannot speak through media discourses. The discussion in this book emphasizes that the medium of film provides a more efficient space for peripheral subjectivities to be reflected. Together,

Mustang, *Tereddüt* and *Yozgat Blues* acknowledge the totalizing practices in peripheral culture—especially male domination—and offer strategies for resistance in different ways. *Mustang* employs the gaze of an enlightened, feminist self at the center, raising the consciousness of the peripheral women to lay the ground for resistance. *Tereddüt* challenges the boundaries between the enlightened self at the center and the disempowered peripheral other, focusing on the mutualities in different women's subordination. *Yozgat Blues* radically demystifies the authority attributed to the centered self by pointing to the possible ways in which the periphery can show its strength and autonomy through diverse gendered experiences.

On the other hand, televisual discourses offer authoritative views on the periphery. Whereas the medium of film problematizes the periphery and provides ways to reflect the peripheral other, military television series suppress peripheral voices. Although the main theme of these series relies on Turkey's Kurdish-populated regions, it is not possible to encounter the reflections of locals regarding their demands for cultural rights, which constitute the root of the long-running Kurdish problem. Rather, Kurdish individuals are defined as people loyal to the state, as their homelands are imagined as exotic geographies in an Orientalist manner. The periphery is the cultural other that the center attempts to save from an enemy figure. The center's superior self is constituted by means of the mainstream worldviews of secular Turks, who tend to reformulate their presence at society's center in light of recent political developments that occurred after 2015.

A similar center–periphery dichotomy is reproduced by THY advertisements, which stereotype the peripheral other in an Orientalist way. In a similar way to the military television series, where armed forces travel to the country's peripheral towns to emancipate the cultural other from oppression, advertisements illustrate how a national brand brings technology and modernity to the underdeveloped other in the periphery. In this regard, the pilot in the THY adverts acts in a similar way to Yavuz in *The Promise*, Fatih in *The Nameless* and Halil *in The Warrior*. The child saluting the THY airplane resembles the locals in the military television series who are loyal to the state. Strikingly, this hierarchizing is conducted by a brand affiliated to the government that defines itself as a representative of the periphery. The lifestyles portrayed by advertisements and television series continue to be dominated by secularist signifiers, rather than Islamic or conservative ones, despite the long reign of a conservative government since 2002. Therefore, the field of cultural production in terms of these media discourses are largely conducted with certain representations that reproduce the Republican ideology's relationship with the periphery as the non-modern, cultural other. Despite the political power achieved by conservative social classes, the advertisements and television series show that they are still underrepresented in popular culture, or as the THY advertisements point at, they cannot coherently figure out how to represent their centered self vis-à-vis the periphery without mimicking Republican ideology.

Finally, *Misvak* cartoons illustrate the ways in which the peripheral individual, who participates in the creation of meaning in the sphere of humor magazines, tends to define his/her existence through establishing new cultural others—a process which points to a crisis of representation in government-affiliated social classes. This inadequate representation by the new participants of the center may be because the conservative social classes possess insufficient *cultural capital* in Pierre Bourdieu's (1984, 1986) terms. Since popular/visual culture—including advertisements and cartoons—is dominated by society's secularist or leftist social classes, the conservative class struggles to initiate adequate dialogue to promote its autonomous and unique self through a habitus that reflects its distinct *taste* in the field of media representations. As an outcome, *Misvak* relies on hostile and discriminating discourses of misogyny, militarism, homophobia and speciesism, and struggles to be distinct from other social classes.

Representations of the periphery in visual culture highlight the narratives put forward by the privileged agents of our society who hold the necessary means to speak for themselves. Yet one definitely has to draw attention to the ones who are deprived of the means to be heard. This includes lower-class citizens living in urban and rural areas, constituting the peripheral population of various cultural, ethnic or religious identities, who cannot get space to produce media discourses. In a similar vein, Turkey's non-Muslim populations, refugees and LGBT+ individuals lack adequate representation in popular culture. Apart from a couple of films that problematize Turkey's issues with regard to multi-culturalism, the mainstream televisual discourse is to a large extent devoid of any signifiers that would provide a certain visibility for ethnic, classed and sexual pluralities. Future research that will explore this subject can build on the arguments in this book, pointing out the dynamic relations between social classes with regard to the technologies of power and, accordingly, contributing to the debate in Turkish media and cultural studies.

BIBLIOGRAPHY

Bourdieu, P. (1984). *Distinction: A Social Critique of the Judgement of Taste.* Cambridge, MA: Harvard University Press.

Bourdieu, P. (1986). The Forms of Capital. In J. Richardson (Ed.), *Handbook of Theory and Research for the Sociology of Education* (pp. 241–258). Westport: Greenwood.

Bibliography

Açar, M. (2015, October 23). Bir Özgürlük Çığlığı [A Cry of Freedom]. Retrieved from http://www.haberturk.com/yazarlar/mehmet-acar/1143761-bir-ozgurluk-cigligi

Ahiska, M. (2010). *Occidentalism in Turkey: Questions of Modernity and National Identity in Turkish Radio Broadcasting*. London/New York: I.B. Tauris.

Akgül, E. (2015, October 29). Map of Media Ownership in Turkey. Retrieved from http://m.bianet.org/english/media/168745-map-of-media-ownership-in-turkey

Akser, M., & Bayrakdar, D. (2014). *New Cinema, New Media: Reinventing Turkish Cinema*. Newcastle upon Tyne: Cambridge Scholars Publishing.

Akyel, E. (2014). #Direnkahkaha (Resist Laughter): "Laughter Is a Revolutionary Action". *Feminist Media Studies, 14*(6), 1093–1094.

Aral, E. (2017, March 20). Apoletli dizi seferberliği [A Wave of Military Series]. Retrieved from https://www.evrensel.net/yazi/78701/apoletli-dizi-seferberligi

Aras, U. (2014, August 11). Erdogan Wins Turkey's Presidential Election. Retrieved from http://www.aljazeera.com/news/middleeast/2014/08/erdogan-wins-turkey-presidential-election-2014810172347586150.html

Arat, Y. (2010). Nation Building and Feminism in Early Republican Turkey. In C. Kerslake, K. Öktem, & P. Robins (Eds.), *Turkey's Engagement with Modernity: Conflict and Change in the Twentieth Century* (pp. 38–51). London: Palgrave Macmillan.

Atakav, E. (2012). *Women and Turkish Cinema: Gender Politics, Cultural Identity and Representation*. London: Routledge.

Atam, Z. (2009). Critical Thoughts on the New Turkish Cinema. In D. Bayrakdar (Ed.), *Cinema and Politics: Turkish Cinema and the New Europe* (pp. 202–220). Cambridge: Cambridge Scholars Publishing.

Atay, T. (2013). The Clash of 'Nations' in Turkey: Reflections on the Gezi Park Incident. *Insight Turkey, 15*(3), 39–44.

Atay, T. (2017a, March 29). 'İsimsizler' ya da evet, evet, evet, evet! ['The Nameless' or Yes, Yes, Yes!]. Retrieved from http://www.cumhuriyet.com.tr/koseyazisi/708754/_isimsizler__ya_da_evet__evet__evet_.html

Atay, T. (2017b, April 5). Referandum dizileri [Referendum Series]. Retrieved from http://www.cumhuriyet.com.tr/koseyazisi/713808/Referandum_dizileri.html

Atay, T. (2017c, April 7). 'SÖZ': PKK sana söylüyorum, IŞİD sen anla! ['THE PROMISE': PKK I Am Telling You, ISIS You Understand!]. Retrieved from http://www.cumhuriyet.com.tr/koseyazisi/715501/_SOZ___PKK_sana_soyluyorum__ISiD_sen_anla_.html

Atay, T. (2017d, April 12). 'Yeni Türkiye'ye Kemalist aşı denemesi: 'Savaşçı' [A Kemalist Vaccine Trial on 'New Turkey': 'The Warrior']. Retrieved from http://www.cumhuriyet.com.tr/koseyazisi/718767/_Yeni_Turkiye_ye_Kemalist_asi_denemesi___Savasci_.html?utm_source=partners&utm_medium=gazeteoku.com&utm_campaign=feed

Aviv, E. E. (2013). Cartoons in Turkey – From Abdülhamid to Erdoğan. *Middle Eastern Studies, 49*(2), 221–236.

Axiarlis, E. (2014). *Political Islam and the Secular State in Turkey: Democracy, Reform and the Justice and Development Party.* London/New York: I.B. Tauris.

Aydın, E., & Dalmış, I. (2008). The Social Bases of the Justice and Development Party. In Ü. Cizre (Ed.), *Secular and Islamic Politics in Turkey: The Making of the Justice and Development Party* (pp. 201–222). New York: Routledge.

Azak, U. (2010). *Islam and Secularism in Turkey: Kemalism, Religion and the Nation State.* London/New York: I.B. Tauris.

Bardakci, M., Freyberg-Inan, A., Giesel, C., & Leisse, O. (2017). *Religious Minorities in Turkey: Alevi, Armenians, and Syriacs and the Struggle to Desecuritize Religious Freedom.* London: Palgrave Macmillan.

Baudrillard, J. (1994). *Simulacra and Simulation.* Ann Arbor: University of Michigan Press.

Behrent, M. C. (2013). Foucault and Technology. *History and Technology, 29*(1), 54–104.

Bourdieu, P. (1984). *Distinction: A Social Critique of the Judgement of Taste.* Cambridge, MA: Harvard University Press.

Bourdieu, P. (1986). The Forms of Capital. In J. Richardson (Ed.), *Handbook of Theory and Research for the Sociology of Education* (pp. 241–258). Westport: Greenwood.

Brakel, K. (2016). The Resurfacing Turkish-Kurdish Question and Its Regional Impact. *DGAPkompakt,* (12), 1–6. Retrieved from https://dgap.org/en/think-tank/publications/dgapanalyse-compact/resurfacing-turkish-kurdish-question-and-its-regional

Carkoglu, A., & Kalaycioglu, E. (2009). *The Rising Tide of Conservatism in Turkey*. New York: Palgrave Macmillan.

Çayır, K. (2008). The Emergence of Turkey's Contemporary 'Muslim Democrats'. In Ü. Cizre (Ed.), *Secular and Islamic Politics in Turkey: The Making of the Justice and Development Party* (pp. 62–79). New York: Routledge.

Cevik, N. (2015). *Muslimism in Turkey and Beyond: Religion in the Modern World*. New York: Palgrave Macmillan.

Çınar, M. (2008). The Justice and Development Party and the Kemalist Establishment. In Ü. Cizre (Ed.), *Secular and Islamic Politics in Turkey: The Making of the Justice and Development Party* (pp. 109–131). New York: Routledge.

Çınar, M., & Duran, B. (2008). The Specific Evolution of Contemporary Political Islam in Turkey and Its 'Difference'. In Ü. Cizre (Ed.), *Secular and Islamic Politics in Turkey: The Making of the Justice and Development Party* (pp. 17–40). New York: Routledge.

Cizre-Sakallioglu, U., & Cinar, M. (2003). Turkey 2002: Kemalism, Islamism, and Politics in the Light of the February 28 Process. *The South Atlantic Quarterly, 102*(2), 309–332.

Coban, S. (2013). Turkey's 'War and Peace': The Kurdish Question and the Media. *Critique, 41*(3), 445–457.

Çolak, E. (2016). İslam ile Görsel Mizah: Türkiye'de İslami Mizah Dergiciliğinin Dönüşümü [Islam and Visual Humor: Transformation of the Islamic Humor Magazine Publishing in Turkey]. *Moment Dergi, 3*(1), 228–247.

Coskun, O. (2018, March 21). Pro-Erdogan Group Agrees to Buy Owner of Hurriyet Newspaper, *CNN Turk*. Retrieved from https://www.reuters.com/article/us-dogan-holding-m-a-demiroren/pro-erdogan-group-agrees-to-buy-owner-of-hurriyet-newspaper-cnn-turk-idUSKBN1GX23R

Dizici, T. M. (2017, May 15). İsimsizler: Gençlerden elinizi çekin! [The Nameless: Take Your Hands Off the Youth!]. Retrieved from https://www.birgun.net/haber-detay/isimsizler-genclerden-elinizi-cekin-159566.html

Dorsay, A. (2015, October 23). Görkemli bir kadın filmi, bir çağdaş sinema başyapıtı [A Magnificent Woman Film, a Contemporary Cinema Masterpiece]. Retrieved from http://t24.com.tr/yazarlar/atilla-dorsay/gorkemli-bir-kadin-filmi-bir-cagdas-sinema-basyapiti,13009

Duran, B. (2008). The Justice and Development Party's 'New Politics': Steering Toward Conservative Democracy, a Revised Islamic Agenda or Management of New Crises? In Ü. Cizre (Ed.), *Secular and Islamic Politics in Turkey: The Making of the Justice and Development Party* (pp. 80–106). New York: Routledge.

Erol, M., Ozbay, C., Turem, Z. U., & Terzioglu, A. (2016). The Making of Neoliberal Turkey: An Introduction. In M. Erol, C. Ozbay, Z. U. Turem, & A. Terzioglu (Eds.), *The Making of Neoliberal Turkey* (pp. 1–14). New York: Routledge.

Fortna, B. C. (2010). The Ottoman Educational Legacy. In C. Kerslake, K. Öktem, & P. Robins (Eds.), *Turkey's Engagement with Modernity: Conflict and Change in the Twentieth Century* (pp. 15–26). London: Palgrave Macmillan.

Foucault, M. (1990). *The History of Sexuality Volume 1: An Introduction* (trans: Hurley, R.). New York: Vintage Books.

Foucault, M. (1991). On the Genealogy of Ethics: An Overview of Work in Progress. In M. Foucault & P. Rabinow (Eds.), *The Foucault Reader* (pp. 372–340). Harmondsworth: Penguin.

Foucault, M. (1995). *Discipline and Punish: The Birth of the Prison* (trans: Sheridan, A.). New York: Vintage Books.

Göle, N. (1996). *The Forbidden Modern: Civilization and Veiling*. Ann Arbor: University of Michigan Press.

Göle, N. (1997). The Gendered Nature of the Public Sphere. *Public Culture, 10*(1), 61–81.

Gümüş, B., & Dural, A. B. (2012). Othering Through Hate Speech: The Turkish-Islamist (V)AKIT Newspaper as a Case Study. *Turkish Studies, 13*(3), 489–507.

Gunter, M. (2008). *The Kurds Ascending: The Evolving Solution to the Kurdish Problem in Iraq and Turkey*. New York: Palgrave Macmillan.

Gürbilek, N. (2011). *Vitrinde Yaşamak: 1980'lerin Kültürel İklimi* [The New Cultural Climate in Turkey: Living in a Shop Window]. Istanbul: Metis.

Gürcan, E. C., & Peker, E. (2015). *Challenging Neoliberalism at Turkey's Gezi Park: From Private Discontent to Collective Class Action*. New York: Palgrave Macmillan.

Heper, M. (2007). *The State and Kurds in Turkey: The Question of Assimilation*. Basingstoke/New York: Palgrave Macmillan.

Hurd, E. S. (2009). *The Politics of Secularism in International Relations*. Princeton: Princeton University Press.

Hurtas, S. (2015, June 10). New Turkish Parliament to Be More Inclusive. Retrieved from https://www.al-monitor.com/pulse/originals/2015/06/turkey-elections-changing--portrait-of-new-parliament.html

Islam, M. K. (2010). *Headscarf Politics in Turkey: A Postcolonial Reading*. New York: Palgrave Macmillan.

Jenkins, G. (2008). *Political Islam in Turkey: Running West, Heading East?* New York: Palgrave Macmillan.

Jones, E. (2016, May 12). Mustang Movie Channels Female 'Power'. Retrieved from http://www.bbc.com/news/entertainment-arts-36225698

Karanfil, G. (2006). Becoming Undone: Contesting Nationalisms in Contemporary Turkish Popular Cinema. *National Identities, 8*(1), 61–75.

Karasipahi, S. (2008). *Muslims in Modern Turkey: Kemalism, Modernism and the Revolt of the Islamic Intellectuals*. New York: I.B. Tauris.

Kardaş, T., & Balci, A. (2016). Inter-Societal Security Trilemma in Turkey: Understanding the Failure of the 2009 Kurdish Opening. *Turkish Studies, 17*(1), 155–180.

Kaya, A. (2013). *Europeanization and Tolerance in Turkey: The Myth of Toleration*. London/New York: Palgrave Macmillan.

Kılınçarslan, C. (2017, March 28). Üç "Terörle Mücadele" Dizisi Gösterimde: Neden Reyting mi? Siyaset mi? [Three "War on Terror" Series Broadcasting: Is Is Rating? Politics?]. Retrieved from https://m.bianet.org/bianet/siyaset/184930-uc-terorle-mucadele-dizisi-gosterimde-neden-reyting-mi-siyaset-mi

Koçer, S. (2013). Making Transnational Publics: Circuits of Censorship and Technologies of Publicity in Kurdish Media Circulation. *American Ethnologist*, 40(4), 721–733. https://doi.org/10.1111/amet.12050.

Koçer, S. (2014). Kurdish Cinema as a Transnational Discourse Genre: Cinematic Visibility, Cultural Resilience, and Political Agency. *International Journal of Middle East Studies*, 46(3), 473–488.

Koksal, O. (2016). *Aesthetics of Displacement: Turkey and Its Minorities on Screen*. London/New York: Bloomsbury Publishing.

Köylü, H. (2017, February 22). TSK'da başörtüsü yasağı kalktı [Veil Ban Lifted in the Army]. Retrieved from http://www.dw.com/tr/tskda-ba%C5%9F%C3%B6rt%C3%BCs%C3%BC-yasa%C4%9F%C4%B1-kalkt%C4%B1/a-37665858

Kural, N. (2015, October 24). Evrensele ulaştı ama yerele hitap edecek mi? [It Reached the Universal But Will It Access the Local?]. Retrieved from http://www.milliyet.com.tr/evrensele-ulasti-ama-yerele-hitap/nil-kural/cumartesi/yazardetay/24.10.2015/2136866/default.htm

Kuzmanovic, D. (2012). *Refractions of Civil Society in Turkey*. New York: Palgrave Macmillan.

Lüküslü, D. (2016). Creating a Pious Generation: Youth and Education Policies of the AKP in Turkey. *Southeast European and Black Sea Studies*, 16(4), 637–649.

Mardin, Ş. (1971). Ideology and Religion in the Turkish Revolution. *International Journal of Middle East Studies*, 2(3), 197–211.

Mardin, Ş. (1973). Center-Periphery Relations: A Key to Turkish Politics? *Daedalus*, 102(1), 169–190.

Mardin, Ş. (2005). Turkish Islamic Exceptionalism Yesterday and Today: Continuity, Rupture and Reconstruction in Operational Codes. *Turkish Studies*, 6(2), 145–165.

Mercan, B. A., & Özşeker, E. (2015). 'Just a Handful of Looters!': A Comparative Analysis of Government Discourses on the Summer Disorders in the United Kingdom and Turkey. In A. Yalcintas (Ed.), *Creativity and Humour in Occupy Movements: Intellectual Disobedience in Turkey and Beyond* (pp. 95–115). London: Palgrave Macmillan.

Navaro-Yashin, Y. (2002). The Market for Identities: Secularism, Islamism, Commodities. In D. Kandiyoti & A. Saktanber (Eds.), *Fragments of Culture: The Everyday of Modern Turkey* (pp. 221–253). New Jersey: Rutgers University Press.

Öncü, A. (1995). Packaging Islam: Cultural Politics on the Landscape of Turkish Commercial Television. *Public Culture, 8*(1), 51–71.

Öncü, A. (1999). Istanbulites and Others: The Cultural Cosmology of 'Middleness' in the Era of Neo-liberalism. In Ç. Keyder (Ed.), *Istanbul: Between the Global and the Local* (pp. 95–119). New York: St. Martins.

Öncü, A. (2000). The Banal and the Subversive: Politics of Language on Turkish Television. *European Journal of Cultural Studies, 3*(3), 296–318.

Öncü, A. (2002). Global Consumerism, Sexuality as Public Spectacle, and the Cultural Remapping of Istanbul in the 1990s. In A. S. Deniz Kandiyoti (Ed.), *Fragments of Culture: The Everyday of Modern Turkey* (pp. 171–190). London/New York: I.B. Tauris.

Öncü, A. (2010). Rapid Commercialisation and Continued Control: The Turkish Media in the 1990s. In C. Kerslake, K. Öktem, & P. Robins (Eds.), *Turkey's Engagement with Modernity: Conflict and Change in the Twentieth Century* (pp. 388–402). London: Palgrave Macmillan.

Öniş, Z. (2015). Monopolising the Centre: The AKP and the Uncertain Path of Turkish Democracy. *The International Spectator, 50*(2), 22–41.

Özbek, M. (1991). *Popüler kültür ve Orhan Gencebay arabeski* [Popular Culture and the Arabesk of Orhan Gencebay]. Istanbul: İletişim Yayınları.

Özbudun, E. (2014). AKP at the Crossroads: Erdoğan's Majoritarian Drift. *South European Society and Politics, 19*(2), 155–167.

Rosati, M. (2015). *The Making of a Postsecular Society: A Durkheimian Approach to Memory, Pluralism and Religion in Turkey*. London/New York: Routledge.

Said, E. W. (1979). *Orientalism*. New York: Vintage Books.

Şalo, F. (2017, April 6). Vatan Millet Kumanda [Nation, People and the Remote Control]. Retrieved from http://www.diken.com.tr/vatan-millet-kumanda/

Sanli, S. (2015). *Women and Cultural Citizenship in Turkey: Mass Media and 'Woman's Voice' Television*. London/New York: I. B. Tauris.

Sayan-Cengiz, F. (2016). *Beyond Headscarf Culture in Turkey's Retail Sector*. London/New York: Palgrave Macmillan.

Şener, Ö. (2013). The Gezi Protests, Polyphony and 'Carnivalesque Chaos'. *Journal of Global Faultlines, 1*(2), 40–42.

Shields, S. (2013). The Greek-Turkish Population Exchange: Internationally Administered Ethnic Cleansing. *Middle East Report, 43*(267), 2–6.

Sinclair, C., & Smets, K. (2014). Media Freedoms and Covert Diplomacy: Turkey Challenges Europe Over Kurdish Broadcasts. *Global Media and Communication, 10*(3), 319–331.

Smets, K. (2016). Ethnic Media, Conflict, and the Nation-State: Kurdish Broadcasting in Turkey and Europe and Mediated Nationhood. *Media, Culture & Society, 38*(5), 738–754.

Somer, M. (2016). Understanding Turkey's Democratic Breakdown: Old vs. New and Indigenous vs. Global Authoritarianism. *Southeast European and Black Sea Studies, 16*(4), 481–503.

Spivak, G. C. (1988). 'Can the Subaltern Speak?': Revised Edition, from the 'History' Chapter of Critique of Postcolonial Reason. In R. C. Morris (Ed.), *Can the Subaltern Speak? Reflections on the History of an Idea* (pp. 21–78). New York: Columbia University Press.

Stokes, M. (1992). *The Arabesk Debate: Music and Musicians in Modern Turkey*. Oxford: Clarendon Press.

Suner, A. (2009). Silenced Memories: Notes on Remembering in New Turkish Cinema. *New Cinemas: Journal of Contemporary Film, 7*(1), 71–81.

Suner, A. (2010). *New Turkish Cinema: Belonging, Identity and Memory*. London/New York: I.B. Tauris.

Tanrıöver, H. U. (2017). Women as Film Directors in Turkish Cinema. *European Journal of Women's Studies, 24*(4), 321–335.

Toprak, B. (2005). Islam and Democracy in Turkey. *Turkish Studies, 6*(2), 167–186.

Toros, E. (2012). The Kurdish Problem, Print Media, and Democratic Consolidation in Turkey. *Asia Europe Journal, 10*(4), 317–333.

Tremblay, P. (2014, November 4). Caricatures of Erdogan Flood Twitter. Retrieved from https://www.al-monitor.com/pulse/originals/2014/10/turkey-cartoonists-unite-against-erdogan.html

Tuncer, A. Ö. (2016, February 8). Mustang bir Özgürleşme Filmi mi? [Is Mustang an Emancipation Film?]. Retrieved from http://www.5harfliler.com/mustang-bir-ozgurlesme-film-mi/

Ünan, A. D. (2015). Gezi Protests and the LGBT Rights Movement: A Relation in Motion. In A. Yalcintas (Ed.), *Creativity and Humour in Occupy Movements: Intellectual Disobedience in Turkey and Beyond* (pp. 75–94). London: Palgrave Macmillan.

Usta, A. (2015, October 25). Turkish Cartoonists Sentenced to Jail for Insulting Erdoğan. Retrieved from http://www.hurriyetdailynews.com/turkish-cartoonists-sentenced-to-jail-for-insulting-erdogan-80145

Van Bruinessen, M. (1992). Kurdish Society, Ethnicity, Nationalism and Refugee Problems. In P. G. Kreyenbroek & S. Sperl (Eds.), *The Kurds: A Contemporary Overview* (pp. 33–67). London: Routledge.

van het Hof, S. D. (2015). Political Potential of Sarcasm: Cynicism in Civil Resentment. In A. Yalcintas (Ed.), *Creativity and Humour in Occupy Movements: Intellectual Disobedience in Turkey and Beyond* (pp. 30–47). London: Palgrave Macmillan.

Vardan, U. (2015, October 24). Genel resim doğru ama… [The General Picture Is Correct However…]. Retrieved from http://www.hurriyet.com.tr/yazarlar/ugur-vardan/genel-resim-dogru-ama-40005458

Vourlias, C. (2016, October 23). Yeşim Ustaoğlu's 'Clair-Obscur' Wins Top Honors at Antalya Film Festival. Retrieved from http://variety.com/2016/film/global/antalya-film-festival-closing-ceremony-clair-obscur-1201898268/

White, J. B. (2002). The Islamist Paradox. *Fragments of Culture: The Everyday of Modern Turkey* (pp. 191–221).

White, J. B. (2010). Tin Town to Fanatics: Turkey's Rural to Urban Migration from 1923 to the Present. In C. Kerslake, K. Öktem, & P. Robins (Eds.), *Turkey's Engagement with Modernity: Conflict and Change in the Twentieth Century* (pp. 425–442). London: Palgrave Macmillan.

Williamson, J. (1985). *Decoding Advertisements: Ideology and Meaning in Advertising.* London: Marion Boyars.

Yalcintas, A. (2015a). Intellectual Disobedience in Turkey. In A. Yalcintas (Ed.), *Creativity and Humour in Occupy Movements: Intellectual Disobedience in Turkey and Beyond* (pp. 6–29). London: Palgrave Macmillan.

Yalcintas, A. (2015b). Prelude: Occupy Turkey. In A. Yalcintas (Ed.), *Creativity and Humour in Occupy Movements: Intellectual Disobedience in Turkey and Beyond* (pp. 1–5). London: Palgrave Macmillan.

Yavuz, M. H. (2003). *Islamic Political Identity in Turkey.* Cary: Oxford University Press.

Yel, A. M., & Nas, A. (2014). Insight Islamophobia: Governing the Public Visibility of Islamic Lifestyle in Turkey. *European Journal of Cultural Studies, 17*(5), 567–584.

Yesil, B. (2016). *Media in New Turkey: The Origins of an Authoritarian Neoliberal State.* Urbana/Chicago/Springfield: University of Illinois Press.

Yıldız, A. (2008). Problematizing the Intellectual and Political Vestiges. In Ü. Cizre (Ed.), *Secular and Islamic Politics in Turkey: The Making of the Justice and Development Party* (pp. 41–61). New York: Routledge.

Yumul, A. (2010). Fashioning the Turkish Body Politic. In C. Kerslake, K. Öktem, & P. Robins (Eds.), *Turkey's Engagement with Modernity: Conflict and Change in the Twentieth Century* (pp. 349–369). London: Palgrave Macmillan.

Žižek, S. (2001). *Enjoy Your Symptom!: Jacques Lacan in Hollywood and Out.* New York: Routledge.

Zürcher, E. J. (2004). *Turkey: A Modern History.* London/New York: I.B. Tauris.

Index[1]

A
Adıvar, Halide Edip, 5
Advertisement/advertising, 14–16, 18–20, 73–80, 88, 92–94
Akad, Ömer Lütfi, 12
Alienation, 12, 39, 42–45
Althusser, Louis, 33
Anatolia, 2, 3, 5, 7, 28
Ankara, 3, 7, 8, 35, 65, 84
Arabesk, 12, 44, 44n5
Araf [Somewhere in Between], 36
Atatürk, Mustafa Kemal, 3, 5, 64, 84, 85
Authoritarianism, 10, 29

B
Bahçeli, Devlet, 85
Baudrillard, Jean, 77
Bayan Yanı, 81
Black Sea, 28, 29, 34–36, 38, 40
Bourdieu, Pierre, 94

C
Cafcaf, 81
Caricature/caricaturist(s), 80–82, 84, 89, 92
Cartoon/cartoonist(s), 12–13, 15, 16, 18, 20, 80–89, 92, 94
Center-periphery
 conflict, 3–6, 10, 46, 92
 dichotomy, 2–20, 30, 35–41, 46, 75, 89, 93
 distinction, 53, 75
 dynamics, 66
 hierarchies, 20, 92
 relations, 2–3, 5, 8–11, 16, 29, 38, 42, 68
Center, the
 enlightening gaze, 79
 ideological interpellation, 33, 41, 76
 military identity, 66
 modernizing and enlightening gaze of, 79
 privileged and superior gaze, 78

[1] Note: Page numbers followed by 'n' refer to notes.

Center, the (*cont.*)
  self-fulfilment, 55–57
  unified, superior self, 40, 46
  victimization, 54, 58
Ceylan, Nuri Bilge, 12
Class/classes, 9–11, 13, 14, 17, 18, 20, 35, 39, 41, 46, 68, 75, 79–82, 89, 92, 94
  struggle, 94
CNN Türk, 15
Conservative/conservatism
  democrats, 8
  lifestyle, 15, 80
  social classes, 11, 68, 81, 94
Constitutional Court, 7, 10, 50
Consumer society, 14
Coşkun, Mustafa Fazıl, 18–19, 41, 46
Crisis, 16, 55, 63, 64, 79, 89
Cultural other, 2–20, 28–35, 42, 45, 46, 53–55, 57, 62, 67, 68, 72–89, 92–94

D
Demirel, Süleyman, 7
Demirkubuz, Zeki, 12
Demirtaş, Selahattin, 85
Democracy, 3, 8, 9
Democrat Party (DP), 4, 6
Discourse, 2, 30, 34, 51, 72, 92
  advertising, 75
  authoritative realm of, 14
  cultural, 5
  discriminating, 94
  diversity of, 15
  government, 64, 67
  media, 18, 57, 92
  news, 14
  Occidentalist, 84
  official, 13
  Orientalist, 74

  political, 11, 34, 46, 60
  religious, 4, 43
  state, 62
  symbolic, 5
  totalizing, 14

E
Economy, 7, 72
  global, 7
  liberal, 8
  privatization, 7
Eğilmez, Ertem, 12
Erbakan, Necmettin, 7, 8
Erdoğan, Recep Tayyip, 8, 9, 11, 16, 34, 51, 77, 79–82, 84, 85
Ergüven, Deniz Gamze, 18, 28, 29, 46
Ethnicity, 35
European Union (EU), 8, 9

F
Femininities, 18, 19
Feminist/feminism
  critique, 28
  filmmakers, 12, 18, 92
  narratives, 18, 37, 38, 40, 41, 66
Film, 11–13, 15–18, 74, 92–94
  narratives, 18, 28–46
Foucault, Michel, 17, 79
FOX TV, 15, 19, 51, 62

G
Gencebay, Orhan, 12
Gender
  gendered dynamics of center-periphery conflict, 10
  gendered forms of subordination in the periphery, 34
  gendered perspectives, 28–46

gendered relations of power, 29
  inequality, 18
  relations, 18, 29, 34–36
Germany, 82, 83, 87, 88
Gezi
  activism, 34, 81
  Gezi Park, 10, 34
Giresun, 73, 78
Gırgır, 81
Greeks, 35
Gül, Abdullah, 10
Güney, Yılmaz, 12

H
Headscarf
  ban, 9, 10
  controversy, 10
Hegemony
  cultural hegemony, 16
  secularist–leftist hegemony, 82
Homophobia, 82, 85, 89, 94
Hürriyet (newspaper), 57

I
Ideology/ideological, 3–5, 7–11,
  13–15, 33, 36, 41, 43, 44, 46,
  65, 66, 68, 72, 76, 78, 79, 85,
  88, 89, 94
Imaginative geographies, 17
Interpellation, 33, 66, 76
Intersectionality, 35
Iraq, 58
Islam
  Islamic fundamentalism, 14
  Islamic lifestyle, 11, 80
  Islamic signifiers, 40, 68
Israel, 83
Istanbul, 3, 7, 8, 12, 30, 33–35,
  37–42, 44, 45, 53–57, 74, 80, 84

J
Journalism, 14–16
Justice and Development Party (JDP),
  8–11, 14–16, 50, 51, 64, 72, 77,
  79, 80, 88, 89, 92
Justice Party (JP), 7

K
Kanal, D., 15, 19, 51, 57
Karaosmanoğlu, Yakup Kadri, 5
Karay, Refik Halit, 5
Kemalist/Kemalism
  center, 68
  elite, 4
  ideology, 5
  imagination, 5
  modernization, 4
  social class, 68
  subjectivity, 65, 67
Kılıçdaroğlu, Kemal, 84
Kurdish/Kurd/Kurds
  broadcasting, 13
  community, 9, 19, 66
  filmmakers, 19
  geographies, 19
  issue, 9, 19, 50, 51, 56, 61,
    62, 66, 67
  opening, 9, 11, 50
  people, 61, 62, 65
  periphery, 13, 50, 68
  politics, 50, 51, 60
  problem, 19, 56, 61, 65, 66, 93
Kurdistan Worker's Party (PKK),
  9, 50, 51, 58, 65, 82, 83, 86

L
Leman, 81
LGBT+, 85, 94
Liberal Republican Party, 3

M

Male gaze, 18, 31
Mardin, Şerif, 2–6, 8, 17, 58, 66
Masculinities/masculinist, 18, 19, 45–46, 55, 84
Media representations, 11–18, 51, 67, 92, 94
Menderes, Adnan, 6
Migration, 7, 35, 80
Militarism/militarist
  anti-militarist, 65, 66
  discourses, 51
  ideology, 65, 76
  national self, 54, 55, 66
  tendencies, 9
Military coup, 6, 7
Misogyny/misogynist, 80–89, 94
Misvak, 20, 80–89, 82n12, 82n13, 94
Modernization, 2, 4, 9, 10, 44, 78
Motherland Party (MP), 7
Multi-culturalism, 9, 12, 35, 55, 94
Mustang, 18, 28–36, 40, 41, 44–46, 93

N

National Order Party, 7
National self, 11, 53–55, 57–60, 62–64, 67
National sovereignty, 50, 59
National subject, 66
Nationalist/nationalism, 2, 12, 35, 51, 59, 68, 76, 82, 85
New Turkish Cinema, 12
Newspaper, 13, 15, 36, 42, 57, 76, 80, 82, 87, 88
Non-Muslim, 2, 3, 12, 82, 94
NTV, 15

O

Ordu, 73, 78
Orientalism, 17
  self-orientalizing, 20, 67
Ot, 81

Ottoman Empire, 2, 3, 5
Özal, Turgut, 7

P

Patriarchal
  culture, 32
  disciplinary body mechanism, 32
  oppression, 34
  relations, 19, 28, 31
Penguen, 81, 82
People's Democratic Party (PDP), 51, 60, 82, 85
People's Houses, 6
Peripheral
  agents, 13, 15, 19, 55–57, 78
  conditions, 75
  culture, 93
  ideology, 41
  individual, 12, 19, 45, 60, 74, 78–80, 94
  lifestyles, 15, 93
  masculinities, 18, 45–46
  other, 9, 11–15, 55, 56, 60–62, 65–67, 72–73, 79, 80, 93
  populations, 2, 4, 5, 9, 44n5, 94
  resistance, 77–80
  subject, 12, 13, 41, 44n5, 60, 61, 67, 74–79, 88
  subjectivities, 6, 14, 31, 34, 92
  towns, 12, 34, 43, 72, 93
  voices, 93
  woman, 31–38, 40, 41, 46, 93
Political Islam/Islamism/Islamist
  broadcasting, 13
  cartoon magazines, 12, 13, 81, 82
  cartoonists, 20
  rise to center, 6
  self, 82
Popular culture, 16, 79, 80, 88, 89, 94
Power
  hierarchy, 74, 76, 88
  relations, 16, 17, 58, 79–82, 89, 92
Progressive Republican Party, 3

R

Race/racism, 14, 82, 89
Radio, 5, 7, 11, 42
　broadcasting, 11
Religious
　fundamentalism, 4, 10
　lifestyle, 4, 15
Republican era
　center, 5, 7
　cultural capital, 15
　elite, 10, 72, 79
　ideology, 8–10, 13, 79, 85, 94
　regime, 74
　social classes, 11
　subjectivity, 62–67
Republican People's Party (RPP), 3, 4, 6, 82, 84, 85, 88
Resistance/resisting, 3, 28–35, 40, 41, 43, 77–80, 93

S

Said, Edward, 17
Secular/secularism/secularist
　center, 67, 68
　ideology, 13
　imagination, 15
　media, 15
Self and the other, 2, 5, 14, 15, 17, 50–68, 79–80
Sexuality/sexualities, 30–33, 36, 38
Seyfettin, Ömer, 5
Soap operas, 14, 62, 68
Social class
　conservative, 11, 81, 94
　peripheral, 10, 13
　secular, 11, 14, 82, 94
Speciesism/speciesist, 80–89, 94
Spivak, Gayatri, 36, 79
Star TV, 19, 51, 52
Subordination, 18, 28–30, 32, 34, 36, 38–41, 46, 93
Syria, 58, 87

T

Tatlıses, Ibrahim, 12
Tecer, Ahmet Kutsi, 5
Technologies of power, 17, 79, 92, 94
Technologies of the self, 17
Television series, 16, 19, 50–68, 92–94
Television/televisual discourse, 7, 12–15, 17–19, 29, 34, 51, 52, 63, 65–68, 73, 76, 77, 87, 92–94
Tereddüt, 18, 35–42, 44–46, 93
Terror
　terrorism, 50, 51, 56, 62, 67
　terrorist, 19, 52, 54–62, 64–67, 83
Trauma/traumatic/traumatized, 2, 6, 11, 12, 33, 36, 37, 39–41, 53, 58, 63, 65
Turkish
　army, 9, 64
　cinema, 11, 12, 18, 46
　economy, 7, 11, 13, 35, 72
　flag, 53, 61, 75, 76
　history, 8, 9, 12, 53, 54, 72
　language, 11
　nation, 5
　national identity, 19, 50, 51, 57
　nationalism, 2, 35, 82, 85
　national literature, 5
　nation state, 19, 35, 59
　politics, 5, 7, 17, 34
Turkish Airlines (THY), 20, 72–80, 88, 93, 94
Turkish Radio and Television (TRT), 13

U

United Kingdom, the, 82
United States, 15, 59, 62, 82–84, 88
Ustaoğlu, Yeşim, 12, 18, 35–38, 46
Uykusuz, 81
Uzak İhtimal [*Wrong Rosary*], 41

V
Village institutes, 6
Violence, 18, 33, 38
Visual culture, 92, 94
Voyeuristic, 31

W
Welfare Party (WP), 7, 8
West/Western
  anti-Western, 8, 88
  anti-Western sentiment, 11, 62, 82–86
  popular music, 44
White Toros, 85

X
Xenophobic, 82

Y
Yeni Akit, 82
Yeşilçam, 11, 12
Yılmaz, Atıf, 12
Yılmaz, Mesut, 7
Yozgat Blues, 18, 41–46, 93

Z
Žižek, Slavoj, 33

CPSIA information can be obtained
at www.ICGtesting.com
Printed in the USA
LVHW07*1922110518
576868LV00016B/432/P